GW00374629

LITTLE BOOK OF
SUNDERLAND

LITTLE BOOK OF
SUNDERLAND

First published in the UK in 2014

© G2 Entertainment Limited 2014

www.G2ent.co.uk

Printed and bound in Europe

ISBN 978-1-782811-91-6

Contents

Foreword

Sunderland AFC has some of the most dedicated and passionate supporters in the country. People who support Sunderland don't just do so on the day of a match, they live and breathe the football club to the point where lives revolve around it.

I was proud to play for the club and to do so for so long. Now I take pride in having the honour of being the club's ambassador. This is a role that has enabled me to witness first hand the vast amount of great work the club does in the community in the north east and beyond.

This book gives you an at a glance guide to some of the people and events that have shaped Sunderland into the club it has grown into in its long and celebrated history.

Jimmy Montgomery, July 2014

Academy

Sunderland's training ground is called 'The Academy of Light.' It is commonly thought to be amongst the most lavishly appointed training complexes in the country. Opened in 2003 it is a very green facility where rain water is captured in wetland areas and then re-cycled to irrigate the pitches.

Sunderland's Academy have produced some excellent players such as Jordan Henderson, Jordan Pickford, Michael Bridges, George McCartney, Jack Colback, Martyn Waghorn and Grant Leadbitter.

Sunderland have been regular winners of their section at U18 level and reached the semi final of the FA Youth Cup most recently in 2008. Sunderland were winners of that competition in 1967 and 1969 as well as reaching the final in 1966.

Below: *Academy pitch and building*

Allan

James Allan was the Founder of Sunderland AFC. Originally called Sunderland and District Teachers' Association Football Club, Sunderland began life in October 1879. James Allan was a Scottish schoolteacher working in Sunderland. After a visit to Edinburgh he brought back with him some round balls of the sort being used in Scotland for the new game of Association Football, and arranged a meeting which created what is now SAFC at the British Day School (This still stands in Sunderland and is now called The Norfolk Hotel).

James Allan played in the club's earliest games. The first ever game was lost 1-0 but Allan scored twice in the second, a 4-0 win. Astonishingly he later scored 12 in a single match as Castletown were thrashed 23-0. In 1887, however, James Allan fell into dispute with the club, eventually leaving to form a rival club called Sunderland Albion. Albion had some success but was short-lived. Games between Sunderland and Sunderland Albion were so bitterly contested that at one point Allan required eye surgery after being stoned at a match at Sunderland's Newcastle Road ground.

Above: *Anderson, Montgomery and Ashurst*

Anderson & Ashurst

The highest outfield appearance makers in the club's history, Stan Anderson and Len Ashurst played for Sunderland in the 1950s and 60s with Ashurst returning to manage the club in the mid-Eighties.

Known as 'Lennie the Lion', Ashurst was the sort of full back who didn't believe in taking prisoners. He was as solid as they come in the tackle and tamed even the greatest of his era's wingers; even George Best never had a good game against him. Capped by England up to U23 level, Ashurst celebrated 50 years in the game in December 2007 when he was still working as a Match Delegate assessing referees in the Barclays Premier League. As a player he had a testimonial at Sunderland and also had testimonials as a manager at both Cardiff City and Newport County who he astonishingly guided to the quarter finals of the old European Cup Winners' Cup.

Stan Anderson was a great Sunderland player of the 1950s and 60s. An England international, he was the first outfield player to top 400 appearances for Sunderland and he remains one of a select club to play for Sunderland, Newcastle and Middlesbrough who he also managed. Stan was a right half, a position that would now be roughly equivalent to the sort of position Roy Keane often played in his heyday. Stan was a class act and the only player to survive when manager Alan Brown broke up Sunderland's unsuccessful band of star names known as the 'Bank of England' team of the Fifties.

Ball

Right: *Kevin Ball in 1999*

Kevin Ball is a legendary figure amongst Sunderland supporters. A blood and thunder player who always gave absolutely everything he had for the cause, Bally captained the side for most of the 1990s, lifting the First Division championship in 1996 and 1999, with a record 105 points on the latter occasion. He has twice served the club in the capacity of caretaker manager/ head coach and has enjoyed a hugely successful coaching career with teams at U18 and U21 level, not least nurturing the talents of England international Jordan Henderson.

'Ooh Bally, Bally' was the chant from the stands whenever Kevin crunched some unsuspecting star opponent. Signed as a centre back from Portsmouth in 1990, Bally became a defensive midfield player, used to shield his back four; a job he did magnificently. A good reader of the game, Bally snuffed out opposition moves effectively and also found time to contribute the occasional goal or telling pass. Perhaps his greatest game came in a 3-0 win over Chelsea when, in addition to subduing Ruud Gullit and co, he scored with a stunning diving header to help him win the 'Man of the Match Award.' A man of the highest professional standards, on and off the pitch, Kevin's stock remains incredibly high with every Sunderland supporter who saw him 'get stuck in' every time he took to the pitch.

Baxter

Slim Jim Baxter was the opposite of Kevin Ball. Whereas Ball wasn't blessed with an overdose of natural talent but proved how to make the absolute best of whatever ability you have, Baxter was a player with the talent to rival George Best but chose to illustrate that ability only when it suited him.

Baxter was on Sunderland's books when he tortured England at Wembley, when Scotland became the first team to defeat the 1966 world champions. Contemptuously performing 'keepie-uppies' in the centre circle as Scotland beat the 'Auld Enemy' 3-2, Baxter showed that he was in a class of his own. His left foot was known as 'The Claw' and he would simply say to team mates that if they made a run forward he would make sure the ball was there when they got there – and he could do that. The trouble was that such performances were on Baxter's terms. Like Len Shackleton before him he was a virtuoso in a team game and the team didn't always benefit as it should have from his talent. A man over-fond of the high life for a professional athlete, his sporadic application frustrated the closely knit team he joined and the team spirit unravelled as a result. Judged on talent alone Baxter should be in any all time team but the tragedy is that at Sunderland the best of Baxter was too rarely seen.

Bennett

Gary Bennett joined Sunderland in 1984, signing for his former Cardiff manager Len Ashurst. 'Benno' wasted no time in endearing himself to the fans, scoring against England 'keeper Peter Shilton within two minutes of his debut. It was the first of 443 games for the Lads placing him fifth on Sunderland's all time appearances list.

Bennett played three times at Wembley for Sunderland: the 1985 League Cup final, the 1990 Play Off final and the 1992 FA Cup final. Sunderland failed to score in any of those matches and Bennett was unfortunate enough to see the only goal of the 1990 Play Off final deflect in off him. The 11 years Gary spent at Sunderland were far from

glorious in the main despite those cup runs, but throughout that time Bennett was a constant presence, mainly at centre half. A commanding player and skipper, Gary led by example, his swashbuckling runs out of defence being a highlight of his era.

Finishing his career in the lower leagues, he had a spell as manager of Darlington but although Manchester born, like so many before him, he found he'd left his heart not in San Francisco but Sunderland, returning to the north east to live and still follow the lads in his role as a BBC Radio summariser.

Above: *Bill Hogg and a teamate with a black cat in 1909*

Black Cats

Synonymous with red and white stripes while their rivals from up the road sport black and white, it puzzles many from outside the north east as to why Sunderland are known as the Black Cats. In fact the black shorts and socks of Sunderland's strip shouldn't be forgotten but the origins of SAFC's nickname are older than the club itself.

Seventy-four years before the formation of the club in 1879, a soldier from the Sunderland Loyal Volunteers was on duty at a gun battery situated at one of Sunderland's two piers at Roker. Perhaps a visit to one of the town's many hostelries preceded his shift but upon hearing painful wailing from outside the gun battery he believed it to be coming

from the devil. In fact the noise proved to be not from the devil but a black cat, after which the battery became known locally as the 'Black Cat Battery.'

There is no record of the football team being associated with black cats when it was formed in 1879 but following the move to Roker Park in 1898 Sunderland are known to have used the black cat as a lucky mascot. In 1905, for instance, the Chairman of the time, F W Taylor, was photographed in a cartoon beside a black cat sat on a football. Ever since then black cats have often appeared on team photographs and match programmes. The Sunderland Supporters' Association have used a picture of a black cat as their emblem ever since their formation

in 1965 and these days the Stadium of Light and the club's administration headquarters' Black Cat House' have huge black cats on their walls.

The nickname the 'Black Cats' was not officially adopted by the club until 2000 and you won't hear fans calling the team 'the black cats' – they call them 'the Lads' but nonetheless Sunderland are proud to be the Black Cats.

Buchan

Charlie Buchan was one of the most famous pre-war players. He was England's centre forward in Wembley's first international in 1924 and is still Sunderland's all time record league goal-scorer. After his playing days Buchan became an eminent broadcaster for the BBC and a famous journalist. In 1951 he created 'Charles Buchan's Football monthly' which became the world's biggest selling football magazine. Buchan didn't stop at football magazines but also published music magazines such as 'Melody Maker' and 'Disc' Indeed he briefly had a young Cliff Richard as his office boy while John Lennon attended one of his parties. Charlie also came up with the idea of The Footballer of the Year award.

However despite his many achievements after he hung his boots up it is as a player that he is mostly and rightly remembered. London born in 1891 he played for Woolwich Arsenal amongst others before moving north to Wearside in 1911. At Sunderland he was top scorer in every season from 1914-15 to 1923-24, being the top scorer in the country in 1922-23. The first of those years as leading scorer saw Sunderland be champions of England and FA Cup finalists.

Right: *Charlie Buchan*

During the First World War he won the Military Medal serving in the Grenadier Guards before joining the Sherwood Foresters. In July 1925 the legendary Herbert Chapman made Charlie his first signing for Arsenal. However he baulked at Sunderland's asking price of £4,000 for a player who was nearly 34. A fee of half that was eventually agreed with the addition that Arsenal would pay Sunderland £100 for every goal Charlie scored in his first season. He ended up costing the Gunners more than the original asking price as he netted 21!

A highly skilful player with good ball control, heading ability and above all intelligence, Buchan only played six times for England despite scoring four times in those games. No doubt he'd have had more caps if he'd spent his best years in the capital rather than the north-east. He also represented The Football league 10 times and was an FA Cup runner up with Arsenal 14 years after being a finalist with Sunderland. His brother Tom played for Bolton Wanderers either side of the Great War.

Canary

Above: *The 1884 Sunderland team*

It is of course Norwich City that are the canaries of football but it is possible that Sunderland are one of those clubs who would have died after a few short years of existence had it not been for a canary.

In 1881, Sunderland were so cash strapped that it looked as if the club might have to fold but thanks to a canary it was saved. Until then the club was still the Sunderland and District Teachers' Association Football Club and in response to the club's financial crisis it was decided to allow non teachers to play and to change the name to Sunderland Association Football Club – S.A.F.C. At the same emergency meeting one of the club's committee members offered his pet canary as a raffle prize. It was duly won by another committee member who offered it again. In the end a sovereign was raised for the bird and the club survived.

Appropriately Sunderland now play at a stadium situated on top of an old coal mine. In days gone past canaries were used in the pits to save lives. If it was feared that there may have been an escape of gas, canaries would be used to test if the air was good. If the poor bird perished then it was known the mine needed to be evacuated immediately. Canaries therefore saved generations of miners in the north east and beyond, and the citadel that now sits atop the biggest mine in the former Durham coalfield stands tall thanks to a canary saving the club before it had ever had a chance to spread its wings and take flight.

Carter

Horatio Stratton Carter was probably the greatest player ever to play for Sunderland. An England international who was joint top scorer in the country with 31 goals when Sunderland won their sixth league title in 1936, he scored the telling second goal in a 3-1 Wembley win over Preston a year later as he captained the Lads to their first ever FA Cup triumph.

Born in Hendon, the birthplace of football in Sunderland, The Raich Carter Centre in Hendon now marks Raich's contribution to football in his home town. A cultured inside forward, Carter was one of England's finest ever players despite losing six of what would have been the best years of his career to World War Two. Having played as a 'Guest' player for Derby during the war he joined them afterwards, helping inspire them to their only FA Cup win in 1946. Carter was the only player to win an FA Cup winner's medal either side of WW2 and for good measure later added an Irish Cup winner's medal in the Fifties when playing for Cork Athletic, more than 20 years since his Sunderland debut.

That came in a 7-4 win over Sheffield Wednesday in October 1932, and a couple of years later he scored four times in another seven-goal haul at Roker Park. This time though it was against England in a trial match when Raich was playing for 'The Rest'. England quickly discovered they couldn't do without him!

Cattermole

Lee Cattermole is a very popular player with Sunderland supporters who like the way 'Catts' gets 'stuck in'. Possibly he has been born in the wrong era because in the modern game you can get a yellow or red card for tackles that 40 years ago might have got you a round of applause rather than a red card. Lee is from Stockton on Teesside and made his name by being a mobile midfielder with immense work-rate combined with a real 'never say die' attitude. Because no player in Sunderland's history has been sent off more times than Lee some people view him as just a destroyer but anyone who watches Sunderland regularly knows that Cattermole can create too.

Never was Cattermoles's value to The Black Cats better illustrated than in the 2013-14 season. Seemingly destined for the drop when seven points adrift of safety with just six games left, Lee lead by example. Three minutes from time in the fifth of those games; with Sunderland's safety mathematically certain as victory over West Brom made it four wins in a row, including wins at Chelsea and Manchester United preceded by a draw at Manchester City, over 45,000 people gave Catts a standing ovation as he limped off injured.

Lee began his career with Middlesbrough winning the Man of the Match award on his debut in a derby at Newcastle as a 17 year old. He went on to appear for 'Boro as a substitute in the

Above: *Lee Cattermole (right) before a match at Arsenal*

2006 UEFA Cup final and at 19 become their youngest ever captain.

He spent a season with Wigan and soon followed his Latics manager Steve Bruce when Bruce took over at Sunderland. Initially partnered in midfield with Albanian international skipper Loric Cana the pair made a fearsomely powerful duo until injury disrupted the partnership. Following Cana's transfer Cattermole took over the captaincy until relinquishing it to John

O'Shea in the summer of 2013 when he evidently was not in head coach Paolo Di Canio's plans. Di Canio however recalled him prior to his departure with Cattermole going on to prove his worth under caretaker boss Kevin Ball and subsequently Gus Poyet for whom he played in the 2014 Capital One Cup final. This was the third final defeat for Lee who was also a runner up in the 2009 European Championships for England at U21 level.

Clough

Famed for his exploits as manager of Nottingham Forest and Derby County, as a player Brian Clough was the quickest to rack up 250 league goals. The first 197 of those came in 213 games for his home town team of Middlesbrough.

A fee of £40,000 brought him north in 1961 when he was at his peak at the age of 26. Clough proceeded to rattle in 54 goals in only 61 league games for Sunderland plus a further nine in 13 cup ties. Hitting 34 goals in his only full season at Roker was impressive but when he damaged his cruciate ligaments on Boxing Day 1962, at home to Bury, Brian already had 28 goals in 28 games that season. Effectively his playing days were over. A comeback was attempted with three games (and one goal) just under two years later but it was in management that his future lay. Beginning as youth coach at Sunderland he moved to Hartlepool, and eventually promotions and league titles at Derby and Forest, adding two European Cups with the latter. Acknowledging his Sunderland manager, Alan Brown, as his mentor, Clough's legacy came back to Sunderland in the form of Roy Keane who Clough nurtured, having brought him into the English game from Cobh Ramblers.

Derby Games

Right:
*Sunderland's
Thomas Sorensen
makes a fine
penalty save from
Alan Shearer*

There are some great derby games in British football: Manchester, Merseyside, North London, Birmingham and Sheffield are amongst those places which can lay claim to a day on their footballing calendars where local rivalry reigns supreme.

What makes derbies in the north east different is that in addition to the renowned reputation of the area as 'the Hotbed of Football' when the striped legions of Wearside and Tyneside meet, it is two football teams representing the pride of two places not two teams from the same place.

Rivalry between Sunderland and Newcastle goes back way beyond the formation of football teams. In the English Civil War Wearside supported the Republican Roundheads of Oliver Cromwell while Royalist Newcastle backed Charles I, and a century later added to their Royalist reputation by backing George II during the Jacobite Rebellion thus earning themselves the moniker 'Geordies.'

Newcastle has always been the commercial capital of the north east but Sunderland is a bigger city and, unlike Newcastle, traditionally a part of County Durham before the creation of 'Tyne and Wear' in 1974. The rivalry between the rival cities finds expression in the derby matches, hence Wear-Tyne derbies being very different affairs to those that take place elsewhere in the country. For the record the biggest victory in the series is also the record away win in any top flight game in English Football: Newcastle United 1, Sunderland 9.

Di Canio

Whether he was knee sliding in celebration at St. James', accepting adulation like a Centurion after beating Everton at the Stadium of Light or pointing to disconsolate fans to keep their chins up at West Brom following what proved to be the last of his 13 competitive games in charge of Sunderland, life was never dull when Paolo Di Canio was around.

As a player Paolo had performed with distinction in a career that began with his favourite club Lazio. He was loaned to Ternana before playing for Juventus, Napoli and AC Milan in his native Italy. A move to Scotland saw his skill and excitable temperament endear him to fans at Celtic prior to a move

across the Roman Wall and south to Sheffield Wednesday where his time at Hillsborough became best known for an incident where he was alleged to have pushed referee Paul Alcock over.

It was at West Ham where Di Canio found his best form. He scored 17 goals in 1999-2000 and 11 the following year with many of these absolute stunners. An overhead trick followed by a fine finish against Arsenal, a sensational volley against Wimbledon and a 30 yard volley in a game against Chelsea, where he scored twice, all saw Hammers fans as giddy as if they were blowing bubbles.

Finishing his playing days in England with Charlton, Paolo returned to Italy to complete his career as a footballer with

Lazio and finally Cisco Roma.

In 2011 he returned to the English game as manager of Swindon with whom he swiftly won promotion and became League Two Manager of the Year in 2012. At Sunderland he was head coach for just under six months spanning two seasons.

Doig

Ted Doig was a goalkeeper who won four league Championship medals at Sunderland before joining Liverpool who he helped to their first two league titles. A Scot who had been a junior with Arbroath at the time of their world record 36-0 win over Bon Accord, Doig became Sunderland's goalkeeper after seven goals were conceded in Sunderland's very first two league games in 1890. Proving that there was no room for sentiment in soccer even then, as long-serving Bill Kirtley was jettisoned and replaced by Doig.

Known as Ned Doig north of the border, Doig made an instant impact keeping a clean sheet on his debut as Sunderland beat WBA 4-0. Unfortunately Doig's registration hadn't been lodged correctly and so Sunderland were docked the very first league points they'd ever won and were fined for good measure. Nonetheless Doig was to prove his worth playing 457 times for Sunderland, a figure only surpassed by two players. In Doig's day Sunderland played as many friendlies as league games each year, such was their appeal as the country's top side. Taking these games into account Doig's total actually approaches 1000 and consequently it may well be Doig, rather than his fellow Sunderland goalkeeper, Jimmy Montgomery, who has actually played most games for the club.

Walk into the foyer of the Stadium of Light and Doig is immortalised along with his team mates from the legendary 'Team

Right: *Ted Doig*

Of All The Talents' from the 1890s, in the world's oldest and biggest oil painting of a soccer match, 'The Corner Kick', by Thomas M M Hemy.

Still the only player ever capped while with Arbroath, Ted Doig played four times for Scotland while with Sunderland, despite the Scots' reticence about capping players with English clubs. The last of those appearances was later declared an unofficial international owing to it being the day of the tragic Ibrox Disaster in which 25 people lost their lives in 1903, the year before he left Wearside.

England

England have played six full internationals at Sunderland at three different grounds. The Stadium of Light was employed for a 2-1 Friendly win against Belgium in 1999 and a crucial Euro 2004 qualifying match with Turkey in 2003, a game which England won 2-0.

Roker Park hosted three full England internationals. A 4-2 win over Wales in 1950, a 2-0 win over Ireland in 1920 and a whopping 13-2 hammering of Ireland in 1899. The first full international played on Wearside was a 4-1 win over Wales at the old Newcastle Road ground in 1891. England therefore have a 100% win ratio from the half dozen games staged at Sunderland with a goal difference of 27-6.

England have also staged many U21, U23 and junior internationals at Sunderland with Football League representative games also being hosted.

Above: *The Stadium of Light*

Europe

The FA Cup win of 1973 took Sunderland into a major European competition for the first time. In those days the now defunct European Cup Winners' Cup was part of a trio of major European competitions flanked by the European Cup (now developed into the Champions league) and the UEFA Cup.

Sunderland kicked off with a handsome 2-0 away win in Hungary where Vasas Budapest were the first opponents. Billy Hughes and Dennis Tueart grabbed the goals, Tueart's after outstripping the home defence with a scintillating dribble from the half way line. Tueart completed an aggregate 3-0 home victory with a penalty in the second leg, in a match where Sunderland

had doubled the usual admission prices apparently to help pay for the new floodlighting required for colour television. So much for the paying fan over the television viewer!

Experienced Portuguese campaigners, Sporting Lisbon, were next up for Bob Stokoe's side who led 2-0 in the home first leg going into the last couple of minutes, courtesy of midfielders, Bobby Kerr and Mick Horswill, only for Hector Yazalde to net a late, late away goal for the visitors. The return in Lisbon was a close fought affair, Sporting edging through 2-0 on the night and therefore 3-2 on aggregate. UEFA reprimanded Sporting afterwards for being unsporting (the ball boys in the vast stadium disappeared the

moment Lisbon lead) but Sunderland's European adventure was over.

Sunderland supporters have long itched for European involvement and when it arrives the enthusiasm for it will be tremendous.

Although a comparatively very minor competition, Sunderland have also participated in the Anglo-Italian competition in 1969-70, 1971-72 and 1992-93 and 1993-94. In the Nineties this only involved qualifying games against domestic opposition but in the Seventies, games were played home and away against Lazio, Fiorentina, Atalanta and Cagliari.

FA Cup

The FA Cup began in 1872, founded by Charles Alcock, a native of Sunderland. In all those years two finals stand out head and shoulders above all others in the national consciousness. One was down to a player and the other down to a team. The final remembered for a player was 'The Matthews final' of 1953 when national hero Stanley Matthews finally got his hands on a winner's medal after twice being a losing finalist. Matthews' Blackpool sensationally recovered from 3-1 down to beat Bolton 4-3 with even a hat trick from South Shields born Stan Mortensen not altering the fact that the game is remembered for and even named after Matthews.

The final remembered for a team was the 1973 FA Cup final when Sunderland created the greatest cup final upset of all. Five months earlier Sunderland had languished fourth from bottom of the old second division. In opposition beneath Wembley's twin towers that rainy day of May 5th 1973 were Leeds United. Managed by former Sunderland forward, Don Revie, Leeds were the FA Cup holders. A year later they would be League champions in the middle of a spell of best part of a decade where they were the country's best side.

They were also the country's most hated side. Their unquestioned talent was overshadowed by what many people viewed as their dirty, underhand and extremely unsporting play. In contrast Sunderland were the nation's darlings – a side boasting one player, schoolboy international Ritchie

Above: *Jimmy Montgomery 1973 FA Cup final save*

Pitt, who had played at Wembley before. Sunderland though had denied Arsenal a third successive year in the final by beating them in the semi and had earlier knocked out cup favourites Manchester City with a performance that summed up the carefree, swashbuckling attacking play that had the biggest and most dormant of the game's sleeping giants well and truly roused.

What's more, Sunderland and Leeds had history, recent history. Sunderland manager Bob Stokoe had alleged that Leeds under Revie had previously tried to get him to throw a game, an allegation against Leeds that Stokoe wasn't the only one to make. In the previous decade two promising young Sunderland talents had broken their legs in games with Leeds, Willie McPheat and

Bobby Kerr, and Kerr was Sunderland's captain now in the final.

Sunderland have always had a love affair with the FA Cup although Lady Luck has rarely smiled in Wearside's direction. At one time it was thought Sunderland were cursed in the cup. Six league titles had been won before the cup was won for the first time when Raich Carter and co beat Preston 3–1 in 1937. Sunderland's first final had been in 1913, a 1–0 defeat at the hands of Aston Villa (before what is still the second biggest crowd ever to watch a match in England) prevented Sunderland from becoming the first team in the twentieth century to do the 'double.' More recently Sunderland were also finalists in 1992, going down 2–0 to Liverpool.

Famous Fans

Below: *Steve Cram is a fan*

Former England cricket captain, Paul Collingwood, Athlete, Steve Cram, 50% of Eurythmics – Dave Stewart, BBC news war reporter, Kate Adie, singer, Imelda May, TV architect, George Clarke, TV & radio presenter, Lauren Laverne, and lyricist, Sir Tim Rice, are all well known fans of Sunderland.

Sportsmen, Collie and Crammie, of course never miss an opportunity to make their red and white allegiance clear. Sir Tim Rice has followed Sunderland since the 1973 FA Cup final and has hosted events for the SAFC Foundation, a charity of which Sunderland born, Kate Adie, is also a stalwart champion, while her fellow Sunderland native, Dave Stewart, has been known to turn up at the match unannounced and incognito just cheering on the lads like everyone else, even if 'Sweet Dreams are Made of This' isn't a song Sunderland fans have been able to sing too often in recent years.

Forster

Picture the scene. Sunderland have just been promoted for the first time in 1964, six years after losing their proud boast of being the only team in the country never to have played outside the top flight of English football. Over 45,000 turn up for the first game of the season against Leicester City. In goal Leicester have Gordon Banks, an FA Cup finalist just over a year earlier and a World Cup winner less than two years in the future, probably England's greatest ever goalie. Meanwhile as the teams line up to kick off, between the sticks at the other end Sunderland have Derek Forster… all 15 years and 185 days of him.

Over four decades later Forster still held the record as the top flight's youngest ever player as well as the record for being the youngest goalkeeper in the entire league. Less than a quarter of the way though the game, fifteen-year-old Forster had twice picked the ball out of his net but Sunderland rallied to draw the game three all. England Schoolboys 'keeper, Forster, kept his place for the next two games as first choice Jimmy Montgomery was injured, but having leaked 10 goals in three games, Sandy McLaughlan was signed to take over. It wasn't until 1968 that Forster was called upon again, coincidentally in a home game with Leicester, but by now he was just a month short of his 19th birthday.

Forster stayed with Sunderland until

Right: *Derek Forster*

after the FA Cup was won in 1973, making a total of just 19 appearances. Derek later played for Charlton and Brighton but destined to remain a reserve made just a combined total of a dozen league appearances for those clubs. Nonetheless a top flight debut at under 15 and a half will forever remain the stuff of comic book fantasies - only Derek Forster actually did it!

Gabbiadini

Marco Gabbiadini was all about pace and power. With thighs like the engines in Ryhope pumping station, Marco simply sped away from defenders as a Ferrari pulls away from a Ford. Combined with his understanding with veteran creator, Eric Gates, Marco was simply a goal waiting to happen. Soon known as 'Marco Goalo,' Gabbiadini took a game to get going, hitting the post on his debut in 1987 after being signed as a teenager from York by his former manager Denis Smith. On the night of Gabbiadini's debut Sunderland sat in their lowest ever league position, 12th in what is now League One. Thankfully Marco scored twice in each of his next three games by which time Sunderland topped the table, as they would come the end of the season.

Within two years Sunderland were back in the top flight, thanks in no small part to the 68th goal Gabbiadini had so far grabbed in Sunderland colours. Newcastle United were the victims of this classic 'G-Force' goal. A play off semi final second leg had four minutes to go when Sunderland doubled their advantage, Gabbiadini latching onto Gates' pass in time honoured fashion and finding the back of the net. Cue pandemonium as Newcastle fans invaded the pitch, cue legendary status on Wearside.

Marco eventually moved on four years and four days after signing. The fee of

Above: *Marco Gabbiadini play off goal v Newcastle*

£1.8m was over 20 times what Sunderland had paid for him. In total Marco scored 87 goals in 185 games for the Lads, the last three coming in a six-minute hat trick just six days before his transfer. Top scorer in each of his four full seasons at Sunderland, Gabbiadini enjoyed a lengthy career totalling 222 league goals in 659 league games excluding a spell in Greece. Sadly he never got the chance to play alongside his brother, Ricardo, whose solitary first team game for Sunderland saw him replace Marco as a sub at Leeds in 1989. For Sunderland supporters though, there was no replacing Marco – even with his brother.

Gurney

Bobby Gurney scored 228 goals for Sunderland in 390 games between 1926 and 1939, making him Sunderland's all time top goalscorer. Gurney's nearest challenger is the great Charlie Buchan whose tally of 222 includes 209 in the league, making Buchan, whose career spanned either side of WW1, Sunderland's top league scorer.

Born in Silksworth, Sunderland in 1907, Gurney scored nine goals for the reserves in his first appearance at Roker Park as a Sunderland player. Bobby was top scorer in a club record seven successive seasons between 1929–30 and 1935–36. In the final year of that sequence Gurney shared the top scorer mantle with Raich Carter with 31 each

Above: *Bobby Gurney*

Gurney also holds the distinction of scoring Sunderland's first ever FA Cup final goal and Sunderland's first at Wembley, his header in the 1937 FA Cup final bringing Sunderland level en route to beating Preston to lift the cup.

Capped once officially by England, Bobby also played and scored for England against Scotland in front of a full house at Hampden Park in an unofficial international. Instead of a cap he was given a loving cup for that appearance. That cup together with his official cap, England shirt, League Championship medal, FA Cup winner's medal, Charity Shield medals and assorted other medals from his career are on display in the entrance hall to the Stadium of Light.

as Sunderland won the league title. It was the second year running Gurney had topped 30 goals and his haul included four in a 7-2 win at Birmingham on the day the championship was clinched.

Guthrie

R on Guthrie was Sunderland's left back in the 1973 FA Cup final. The final was only his 21st appearance for Sunderland after a decade with his home town team of Newcastle. Guthrie though was mainly a reserve at St. James and made eleven fewer league appearances for Newcastle than he did in his two and a half years at Sunderland.

Guthrie was one of a handful of shrewd signings by Bob Stokoe when he came to Sunderland and the full back immediately slotted into the side. Keen to get forward Guthrie went close to scoring in the cup final but did get a cup goal to his name in the 2-0 quarter final win over Luton.

Upon leaving Sunderland two years

after the cup triumph, Ron's FA Cup exploits weren't over despite moving into local non league football, as in 1978 he helped Blyth Spartans to the fifth round of the FA Cup where they eventually lost to Wrexham in a replay at his first home of St. James' Park.

Halliday

With 43 goals in one season Dave Halliday holds Sunderland's record for the most goals in one season, a feat he achieved in 1928-29. It was his fourth and final full season on Wearside. In his three previous terms he'd notched 42, 37 and 39 so it is no surprise that Halliday also holds the best goals per game ratio of any Sunderland player. His tally of 165 goals in 175 games equals 0.943 goals per game. Brian Clough with 0.851 is next highest of those players who played at least 50 games for the club. In fact in Halliday's poorest full season he scored more goals than any other player has ever managed in their best!

Had Halliday been Sunderland's penalty taker in his record breaking season he could have had another 10 goals! Only one of his 43 goals was scored from the spot. That was on the day regular spot-kick specialist Billy Clunas was missing. Clunas scored 10 penalties that season.

Halliday managed four goals in a game three times for Sunderland and a dozen hat tricks. In the history of the game only five players can better Halliday's tally of 347 goals in 464 Football league

and Scottish league appearances although amazingly this goal machine was never capped!

Like Charlie Buchan, Halliday left Sunderland for Arsenal. His stay at Highbury was brief despite the fact that in his final appearance for the Gunners he scored four goals in a 6-6 draw with Portsmouth that still stands as the Football League's highest scoring draw.

Having done so much for Sunderland as a player in the Twenties, three decades later Halliday played a part in one of the club's darkest days. Never relegated until 1958, Sunderland won at Portsmouth on the last day of the 1957-58 season to give themselves a chance of escaping the drop, only to learn that relegation rivals Leicester had also won therefore relegating Sunderland. Halliday was Leicester's manager.

Halom

Centre forward in the 1973 FA Cup winning team, Vic Halom scored twice in the cup run. He opened the scoring in the semi final against Arsenal in which he tormented the Gunners' defence, and in the fifth round replay with Manchester City he smashed home a goal that many Sunderland supporters believe has never been bettered. That thunderbolt came on what was only Halom's fourth appearance for Sunderland. Bob Stokoe had previously managed Halom at Charlton, and Vic was the final piece in Sunderland's jigsaw.

A traditional British targetman, Halom would never fail to 'get his retaliation in first!' His decade was that of the 1970s, the decade when the hard men of British Football: Norman Hunter, Billy Bremner, Peter Storey,

Ron 'Chopper' Harris and co seemingly had a 'licence to kill.' This was decades before the tackle from behind, the two footed lunge and so on were outlawed. It was rough stuff and they didn't come rougher or tougher than Vic. No matter what the game's tough guys were going to dish out though they were going to get plenty back from Halom. Not surprisingly the fans loved him. Far from just a tough customer however, Vic could play and he had the physical attributes to enable his ability to come through. He got the ball in the back of the net in the cup final, typically though Halom put Leeds 'keeper David Harvey in the rigging with it and the 'goal' was disallowed. More profitably it was Halom's knock down from a Billy Hughes corner that led to Ian Porterfield scoring the only goal of the game.

Ha'way the Lads

H a'way the Lads. For readers outside of the north east this simply means 'Come on Sunderland!' It is the battle cry of the 'Hotbed of Soccer'. The renowned Roker Roar still exists at the Stadium of Light. In 2007 Sunderland supporters were officially recognised as the loudest in the country. That came as no surprise.

For generations the heartfelt cry of 'Haaaaaaaaaaway the lads' has urged Sunderland to 'get stuck in' and when Sunderland do that the volume rises accordingly. Sunderland supporters demand the same level of graft from those playing at the Stadium of Light as those once mining the coal seams underneath it were required to give.

The seats at the 'north' end of the Stadium of Light display the words 'Ha'way the Lads.' It is a phrase children of Sunderland supporters learn almost as soon as they learn to say mam and dad.

The Tyneside variation is 'Ho'way the Lads' but at Sunderland it is very much 'Ha'way the Lads' and it always will be.

Below
Sunderland Fans:

Horswill

Micky Horswill was a vital cog in the 1973 FA Cup winning team. Like his fellow flame-headed midfielder on that same Wembley turf seven years earlier – Alan Ball, in the 1966 World Cup final – Horswill was the youngest member of the side and the man who covered the most ground.

Horswill's job was to stop the other team's midfield generals playing. He'd already succeeded in stopping Alan Ball in the semi final with Arsenal, and in the fifth round he'd put the cuffs on Man City's Cold Heseldon-born creative maestro, Colin Bell, and found time to score himself. Beneath the twin towers Horswill had his work cut out. Leeds boasted many of the top stars in Europe, amongst them Billy Bremner and John Giles, in Horswill's central midfield area. With Horswill's fellow midfield runner, Bobby Kerr, detailed with assisting right back, Dick Malone, in dealing with Leeds' dangerman, Eddie Gray, a lot was required of the Annfield Plain lad who was barely 20.

Thankfully Horswill didn't lack horse-power and largely thanks to his endeavours the creative powers of one of the best sides in Europe were kept in check.

When he left for Manchester City in the month he turned 21, Horswill had played just under 100 times for the club he grew up supporting. He played just 14 league games in 16 months in Manchester before moving on to Plymouth, Hull, Happy Valley of Hong Kong, non league Barrow and finally a solitary league appearance for Carlisle a decade after his Cup final appearance took his league tally to 270. It should have been more.

Hughes

" At the moment he's the best forward in Britain" commented Manchester United manager Tommy Docherty after seeing Billy Hughes score twice at Old Trafford in 1974. 'Oh how'd you win the cup?' the United fans were quick to taunt after the Red Devils took an early lead in what 'Match of the Day' were to name as their 'Match of the Season' in 1974-75.

"That's how we won the cup" came the reply from the red and white army a few minutes later by which time Billy Hughes' double strike had put Sunderland ahead. Billy in full flow was a stirring sight. Dark locks flowing behind him and with tanned legs that had his female fans feeling weak at the knees,

Billy was a fantastically exciting player.

In those far away early Seventies, rockers Wishbone Ash twin lead guitars were thrilling crowds at the 'Mecca' mid way between Roker Park and the site that is now the Stadium of Light. Similarly the twin speed merchants on the wings of Roker Park, Hughes and Dennis Tueart, were the most exciting thing Sunderland fans had seen in

Left: *Billy Hughes*

years. Hughesie top scored in the cup winning season, his 19 goals included four in the cup – the winner in the semi final and three in the two games with Man City in the fifth round. Everyone rightly remembers Vic Halom's goal in the replay with City but Billy got a brace in that 3-1 win and it was his corner that Sunderland scored from in the final.

Used just once by Scotland, Billy deserved many more caps. His brother John 'Yogi' won eight. The pair played together just once, on John's only Sunderland appearance. Injury made John's debut also his last. Vic Halom was brought in to replace him and the 'H-bombers' of Hughes and Halom accounted for Man City and Arsenal between them. Some would call it fate.

Hurley

Still revered as 'The King' at Sunderland, Charlie Hurley made his 401st and last Sunderland appearance in 1969. A decade later supporters voted him Sunderland's 'Player of the Century' in marking the club's Centenary. Almost another two decades on 'The King' was invited to dig up the centre spot at Roker Park after the final game at the ground, ready for its transportation to the club's new home at the Stadium of Light. Move the clock on another decade and Hurley's reputation saw him named as Millwall's greatest ever player, become only the second soccer player after John Giles to be inducted into the Irish Sporting Hall of Fame and at Sunderland a sold out event celebrated the 50th anniversary of him joining the club.

Sunderland's most capped player, Charlie won all but the first and last of his 40 Republic of Ireland caps while with the Lads. He captained Sunderland to the club's first ever promotion in 1964, being runner up to West Ham's cup winning captain Bobby Moore as 'Footballer of the Year' in the process.

A cultured defender, who liked to play the ball out of defence when most preferred to see how far they could welly it, Charlie was ahead of his time. On Boxing Day 1960 he became the first centre half to go forward for a corner kick, something every centre back in the world does as routine now, but back then it was unheard of. Hurley equalised in that match against Sheffield United and in the next home match on New Year's Eve he netted again as Luton Town were hammered 7-1. Hurley wreaked such havoc at corners that even if he didn't score himself someone else would be more than likely to score from a rebound if Hurley's effort was blocked.

Just like centre halves going forward for corners was unheard of before Hurley, it was also not the done thing for crowds to chant, but whenever Sunderland got a corner the chant 'Charlie, Charlie' would rise up right around the ground as Hurley moved into the box ready to pass into footballing folklore.

Internationals

CAPS	PLAYER
ENGLAND TOP 5	
14	Dave Watson
11	Arthur Bridgett
10	George Holley
8	Kevin Phillips
6	Charlie Buchan / Raich Carter

It is often felt that playing in the north east has held back the international claims of players, and the meagre totals on some of these lists illustrate that point. It still staggers anyone who watched England lose their World Champions crown in 1970 when Gordon Banks missed the quarter final through injury, that the back up was not Jimmy Montgomery. Yes Sunderland had been relegated that season but Monty had been magnificent. Instead Sir Alf Ramsay took Peter Bonetti of cup winners Chelsea and Man Utd's Alex Stepney. Monty remained uncapped, the nearest he got being an unused sub against France in 1969. Nonetheless Jim still made the best save ever seen at Wembley!

Sunderland's first international was right back, Tom Porteous, who won his solitary England cap when England beat Wales 4-1 in Sunderland on March 7th 1891. Seaham-born, George Holley, scored eight goals in his 10 games to be Sunderland's highest scorer for England. The last Sunderland player to score for England was Len Shackleton who scored a brilliant individual goal against World Champions West Germany in 1954 but was never picked again!

Half backs are Sunderland's most capped players for three of the four home countries and the Republic of Ireland. Centre halves Charlie Hurley, Dave Watson, Andy Melville and Martin Harvey who mainly operated at right half.

CAPS	PLAYER
SCOTLAND TOP FIVE	
17	Craig Gordon
13	Phil Bardsley
10	Jim Baxter
9	Charlie Thomson
9	Allan Johnston
WALES TOP 5	
17	Andy Melville
13	Trevor Ford
13	David Vaughan
10	John Oster
9	L.R. Roose / Ray Daniel

CAPS	PLAYER
N.I TOP FIVE	
34	Martin Harvey
33	Billy Bingham
20	George McCartney
13	Phil Gray
12	Johnny Crossan / Jeff Whitley
R.O.I TOP 5	
38	Charlie Hurley
37	Kevin Kilbane
31	Niall Quinn
25	John O'Shea
12	Paul McShane
OVERSEAS TOP 5	
32	Seb Larsson, Sweden
30	Cristian Riveros, Paraguay
27	Thomas Sorensen, Denmark
21	Paulo Da Silva, Paraguay
19	Marton Fulop, Hugary

Trevor Ford has most international goals to his name while with Sunderland, the Fifties forward scoring 12 times in the 13 games he played for Wales while with Sunderland, the first two of those goals coming at Roker Park against England in 1950. Sunderland's Willie Watson was in the England side for that game. He won all four of his caps while with Sunderland but also played another 23 games for his country – at cricket!

Ireland

Right: *Billy Bingham*

Sunderland have long had a strong bond with Ireland. Cork-born, Charlie Hurley, was voted Player of the Century in 1979 and remains the club's most capped international. Raich Carter won cups with both Sunderland and Cork Athletic either side of WW2 and Northern Ireland internationals, Billy Bingham and Martin Harvey, both gave distinguished service to club and country.

In 2006 Dublin-born Niall Quinn became Chairman of the club. The Republic of Ireland's all time top scorer at the time of his retirement, he'd scored the last seven of his 21 international goals while a Sunderland player. Quinn assembled a mainly Irish based group of backers called The Drumaville Consortium to buy the club and give it a new direction.

Recent years have seen Sunderland's links with the emerald isle further strengthened, not least through the periods when Roy Keane and Martin O'Neill managed the club while of course Mick McCarthy who managed the Republic at the 2002 World Cup subsequently became a trophy winning manager at Sunderland three years later.

John O'Shea has captained both Sunderland and the Republic of Ireland with distinction whilst David Meyler, James McClean, Paul McShane, Liam Miller, Daryl Murphy and Anthony Stokes are amongst others to have represented the Republic as Sunderland players in the modern era.

Keane

Reckoned by many experts to be the best midfielder in the world when at his peak with Manchester United and the Republic of Ireland, Roy Keane strode the global game as a giant.

The game is littered with great players who failed to become great managers but given a first opportunity at Sunderland Keane made a sensational start. Twenty-third in the Championship when he took over, he signed six players in the day or two that remained until the transfer window slammed shut, proceeded to start with two away wins and come the end of the season the Championship trophy was secured.

Roy Keane managed Sunderland from August 28th 2006 to December 4th 2008. He was in charge for exactly 100 competitive games winning two more than he lost, 43 to 41.

Below: *Roy Keane congratulates Stephen Wright*

Kerr

Captain of the 1973 FA Cup winning team, Bobby Kerr played 433 games for Sunderland between New Year's Eve 1966 and August 1978 scoring 69 goals. Only five men have played more games for the Lads than this Scot.

Arriving at the club as a 16-year-old in the summer of 1963, Bobby burst onto the scene as a teenager scoring seven goals in his first 11 games including two against Newcastle before breaking his leg in an FA Cup tie with Leeds. Kerr broke his leg a second time before working his way back to fitness. It was fairytale stuff when on May 5th 1973 all 5'4" of the midfielder who manager Bob Stokoe

called his 'Little General', held the cup aloft having defeated Leeds United at Wembley and having fully deserved to do so.

Consistency was Kerr's key. He covered immense ground as the chant fans' dedicated to him illustrated: 'He's here, he's there he's every★★★★★★ where, Bobby Kerr, Bobby Kerr.' In the six seasons Sunderland spent out of the top flight in the early Seventies, Kerr missed only eight games. He retained his early eye for goal, probably his most spectacular being a stunning goal at Birmingham in 1971 when positioned on the edge of the box he met a corner full on the volley and smashed it home.

League Positions

No.	Season	Division	Final Position	No. of games	Home Win	Home Draw	Home Loss	Home For	Home Against	Away Win	Away Draw	Away Loss	Away For	Away Against	Goals Scored	Points
1	1890/91	One	7	22	7	2	2	31	13	3	3	5	20	18	51	23
2	1891/92	One	1	26	13	0	0	55	11	8	0	5	38	25	93	42
3	1892/93	One	1	30	13	2	0	58	17	9	2	4	42	19	100	48
4	1893/94	One	2	30	11	3	1	46	14	6	1	8	26	30	72	38
5	1894/95	One	1	30	13	2	0	51	14	8	3	4	29	23	80	47
6	1895/96	One	5	30	10	5	0	36	14	5	2	8	16	27	52	37
7	1896/97	One	15	30	4	6	5	21	21	3	3	9	13	26	34	23
8	1897/98	One	2	30	12	2	1	27	8	4	3	8	16	22	43	37
9	1898/99	One	7	34	11	3	3	26	10	4	3	10	15	31	41	36
10	1899/1900	One	3	34	12	2	3	27	9	7	1	9	23	26	50	41
11	1900/01	One	2	34	12	3	2	43	11	3	10	4	14	15	57	43
12	1901/02	One	1	34	12	3	2	32	14	7	3	7	18	21	50	44
13	1902/03	One	3	34	10	5	2	27	11	6	4	7	24	25	51	41

No.	Season	Division	Final Position	No. of games	Home Win	Home Draw	Home Loss	Home For	Home Against	Away Win	Away Draw	Away Loss	Away For	Away Against	Goals Scored	Points
14	1903/04	One	6	34	12	3	2	41	15	5	2	10	22	34	63	39
15	1904/05	One	5	34	11	3	3	37	19	5	5	7	23	25	60	40
16	1905/06	One	14	38	13	2	4	40	21	2	3	14	21	49	61	35
17	1906/07	One	10	38	10	4	5	42	31	4	5	10	23	35	65	37
18	1907/08	One	16	38	11	2	6	53	31	5	1	13	25	44	78	35
19	1908/09	One	3	38	14	0	5	41	23	7	2	10	37	40	78	44
20	1909/10	One	8	38	12	3	4	40	18	6	2	11	26	33	66	41
21	1910/11	One	3	38	10	6	3	44	22	5	9	5	23	26	67	45
22	1911/12	One	8	38	10	6	3	37	14	4	5	10	21	37	58	39
23	1912/13	One	1	38	14	2	3	47	17	11	2	6	39	26	86	54
24	1913/14	One	7	38	11	3	5	32	17	6	3	10	31	35	63	40
25	1914/15	One	8	38	11	3	5	46	30	7	2	10	35	42	81	41
26	1919/20	One	5	42	17	2	2	45	16	5	2	14	27	43	72	48
27	1920/21	One	12	42	11	4	6	34	19	3	9	9	23	41	57	41
28	1921/22	One	12	42	13	4	4	46	23	3	4	14	14	39	60	40
29	1922/23	One	2	42	15	5	1	50	25	7	5	9	22	29	72	54
30	1923/24	One	3	42	12	7	2	38	20	10	2	9	33	34	71	53
31	1924/25	One	7	42	13	6	2	39	14	6	4	11	25	37	64	48
32	1925/26	One	3	42	17	2	2	67	30	4	4	13	29	50	96	48
33	1926/27	One	3	42	15	3	3	70	28	6	4	11	28	42	98	49
34	1927/28	One	15	42	9	5	7	37	29	6	4	11	37	47	74	39
35	1928/29	One	4	42	16	2	3	67	30	4	5	12	26	45	93	47
36	1929/30	One	9	42	13	3	5	50	35	5	4	12	26	45	76	43
37	1930/31	One	11	42	12	4	5	61	38	4	5	12	28	47	89	41
38	1931/32	One	13	42	11	4	6	42	29	4	6	11	25	44	67	40
39	1932/33	One	12	42	8	7	6	33	31	7	3	11	30	49	63	40

Right: *Sunderland Fans*

No.	Season	Division	Final Position	No. of games	Home Win	Home Draw	Home Loss	Home For	Home Against	Away Win	Away Draw	Away Loss	Away For	Away Against	Goals Scored	Points
40	1933/34	One	6	42	14	6	1	57	17	2	6	13	24	39	81	44
41	1934/35	One	2	42	13	4	4	57	24	6	12	3	33	27	90	54
42	1935/36	One	1	42	17	2	2	71	33	8	4	9	38	41	109	56
43	1936/37	One	8	42	17	2	2	59	24	2	4	15	30	63	89	44
44	1937/38	One	8	42	12	6	3	32	18	2	10	9	23	39	55	44
45	1938/39	One	16	42	7	7	7	30	29	6	5	10	24	38	54	38
46	1946/47	One	9	42	11	3	7	33	27	7	5	9	32	39	65	44
47	1947/48	One	20	42	11	4	6	33	18	2	6	13	23	49	56	36
48	1948/49	One	8	42	8	10	3	27	19	5	7	9	22	39	49	43
49	1949/50	One	3	42	14	6	1	50	23	7	4	10	33	39	83	52
50	1950/51	One	12	42	8	9	4	30	21	4	7	10	33	52	63	40
51	1951/52	One	12	42	8	6	7	41	28	7	6	8	29	33	70	42
52	1952/53	One	9	42	11	9	1	42	27	4	4	13	26	55	68	43
53	1953/54	One	18	42	11	4	6	50	37	3	4	14	31	52	81	36

No.	Season	Division	Final Position	No. of games	Home Win	Home Draw	Home Loss	Home For	Home Against	Away Win	Away Draw	Away Loss	Away For	Away Against	Goals Scored	Points
54	1954/55	One	4	42	8	11	2	39	27	7	7	7	25	27	64	48
55	1955/56	One	9	42	10	8	3	44	36	7	1	13	36	59	80	43
56	1956/57	One	20	42	9	5	7	40	30	3	3	15	27	58	67	32
57	1957/58	One	21	42	7	7	7	32	33	3	5	13	22	64	54	32
58	1958/59	Two	15	42	13	4	4	42	23	3	4	14	22	52	64	40
59	1959/60	Two	16	42	8	6	7	35	29	4	6	11	17	36	52	36
60	1960/61	Two	6	42	12	5	4	47	24	5	8	8	28	36	75	47
61	1961/62	Two	3	42	17	3	1	60	16	5	6	10	25	34	85	53
62	1962/63	Two	3	42	14	5	2	46	13	6	7	8	38	42	84	52
63	1963/64	Two	2	42	16	3	2	47	13	9	8	4	34	24	81	61
64	1964/65	One	15	42	12	6	3	45	26	2	3	16	19	48	64	37
65	1965/66	One	19	42	13	2	6	36	28	1	6	14	15	44	51	36
66	1966/67	One	17	42	12	3	6	39	26	2	5	14	19	46	58	36
67	1967/68	One	15	42	8	7	6	28	28	5	4	12	23	33	51	37
68	1968/69	One	17	42	10	6	5	28	18	1	6	14	15	49	43	34
69	1969/70	One	21	42	4	11	6	17	24	2	3	16	13	44	30	26
70	1970/71	Two	13	42	11	6	4	34	21	4	6	11	18	33	52	42
71	1971/72	Two	5	42	11	7	3	42	24	6	9	6	25	33	67	50
72	1972/73	Two	6	42	12	6	3	35	17	5	6	10	24	32	59	46
73	1973/74	Two	6	42	11	6	4	32	15	8	3	10	26	29	58	47
74	1974/75	Two	4	42	14	6	1	41	8	5	7	9	24	27	65	51
75	1975/76	Two	1	42	19	2	0	48	10	5	6	10	19	26	67	56
76	1976/77	One	20	42	9	5	7	29	16	2	7	12	17	38	46	34
77	1977/78	Two	6	42	11	6	4	36	17	3	10	8	31	42	67	44
78	1978/79	Two	4	42	13	3	5	39	19	9	8	4	31	25	70	55
79	1979/80	Two	2	42	16	5	0	47	13	5	7	9	22	29	69	54

LEAGUE POSITIONS

No.	Season	Division	Final Position	No. of games	Home Win	Home Draw	Home Loss	Home For	Home Against	Away Win	Away Draw	Away Loss	Away For	Away Against	Goals Scored	Points
80	1980/81	One	17	42	10	4	7	32	19	4	3	14	20	34	52	35
81	1981/82	One	19	42	6	5	10	19	26	5	6	10	19	32	38	44
82	1982/83	One	16	42	7	10	4	30	22	5	4	12	18	39	48	50
83	1983/84	One	13	42	8	9	4	26	18	5	4	12	16	35	42	52
84	1984/85	One	21	42	7	6	8	20	26	3	4	14	20	36	40	40
85	1985/86	Two	18	42	10	5	6	33	29	3	6	12	14	32	47	50
86	1986/87	Two	20	42	8	6	7	25	23	4	6	11	24	36	49	48
87	1987/88	Three	1	46	14	7	2	51	22	13	5	5	41	26	92	93
88	1988/89	Two	11	46	12	8	3	40	23	4	7	12	20	37	60	63
89	1989/90	Two	6	46	10	8	5	41	32	10	6	7	29	32	70	74
90	1990/91	One	19	38	6	6	7	15	16	2	4	13	23	44	38	34
91	1991/92	Two	18	46	10	8	5	36	23	4	3	16	25	42	61	53
92	1992/93	New One	21	46	9	6	8	34	28	4	5	14	16	36	50	50
93	1993/94	New One	12	46	14	2	7	35	22	5	6	12	19	35	54	65
94	1994/95	New One	20	46	5	12	6	22	22	7	6	10	19	23	41	54
95	1995/96	New One	1	46	13	8	2	32	10	9	9	5	27	23	59	83
96	1996/97	Premier	18	38	7	6	6	20	18	3	4	12	15	35	35	40
97	1997/98	New One	3	46	14	7	2	49	22	12	5	6	37	28	86	90
98	1998/99	New One	1	46	19	3	1	50	10	12	9	2	41	18	91	105
99	1999/2000	Premier	7	38	10	6	3	28	17	6	4	9	29	39	57	58
100	2000/01	Premier	7	38	9	7	3	24	16	6	5	8	22	25	46	57
101	2001/02	Premier	17	38	7	7	5	18	16	3	3	13	11	35	29	40
102	2002/03	Premier	20	38	3	2	14	11	31	1	5	13	10	34	21	19

SUNDERLAND A.F.C. 1936-37
— LEAGUE CHAMPIONS —

BELL, MIDDLETON, RODGERSON, LOCKIE, W. DUNLOP (ASST TRAINER), McDOWALL, ROBINSON, BRYCE, BURBANKS
MOOR, MURRAY, COLLIN, J. CLARK, SHAW, MAPSON, JOHNSTON, HORNBY, DUNS, SAUNDERS, T. CLARK
JOHN COCHRANE (SEC. MANAGER), RUSSELL, McNAB, GURNEY, CARTER, HASTINGS (CAPT), HALL, WYLLIE, URWIN, A. REID (TRAINER)
DAVIS, THOMSON, GALLACHER, CONNOR

No.	Season	Division	Final Position	No. of games	Home Win	Home Draw	Home Loss	Home For	Home Against	Away Win	Away Draw	Away Loss	Away For	Away Against	Goals Scored	Points
103	2003/04	New One	3	46	13	8	2	33	15	9	5	9	29	30	62	79
104	2004/05	Championship	1	46	16	4	3	45	21	13	3	7	31	20	76	94
105	2005/06	Premier	20	38	1	4	14	12	37	2	2	15	14	32	26	15
106	2006/07	Championship	1	46	15	4	4	38	18	12	3	8	38	29	76	88
107	2007/08	Premier	15	38	9	3	7	23	21	2	3	14	13	38	36	39
108	2008/09	Premier	16	38	6	3	10	21	25	3	6	10	13	29	34	36
109	2009/10	Premier	13	38	9	7	3	32	19	2	4	13	16	37	48	44
110	2010/11	Premier	10	38	7	5	7	25	27	5	6	8	20	29	45	47
111	2011/12	Premier	13	38	7	7	5	26	17	4	5	10	19	29	45	45
112	2012/13	Premier	17	38	5	8	6	20	19	4	4	11	21	35	41	39
113	2013/14	Premier	14	38	5	3	11	21	27	5	5	9	20	33	41	38

League Cup

Sunderland's Wembley appearance in the 2014 Capital One Cup final was their second appearance in the final of the League Cup which was known as the Milk Cup on Sunderland's previous appearance in the final in 1985.

The competition began in 1960, Sunderland's first game being a defeat at Brentford. In the third year of the trophy the Wearsiders reached the semi final for the first time, going down over two legs to Aston Villa.

The semi final stage was also reached in 1999 when Leicester City, managed by future Sunderland boss Martin O'Neill, proved just too strong over two legs.

Sunderland's record win in the competition is a 7-0 away victory at Cambridge United in 2002-03, seven goals also being scored against Oldham Athletic in a 7-1 home win in 1962-63. Derby County inflicted Sunderland's record League Cup defeat, beating the Lads 6-0 in 1990-91 – after Sunderland had won 6-1 away to Bristol City in the second leg of the previous tie.

Brian Clough and Marco Gabbiadini are Sunderland's record league Cup goalscorers with nine goals while Gary Bennett's 35 appearances make him Sunderland's highest appearance maker in the competition, Jimmy Montgomery being the only other player to play in over 30 games.

Nine matches is both the club record for the longest unbeaten run in League Cup games and also the longest number of games without a win.

Legion of Light

Legion of Light is Sunderland AFC's official club magazine. It is posted three times a year to every Sunderland season ticket holder and goes on sale throughout the north east of England.

Being SAFC's own publication 'Legion of Light' boasts unrivalled access to Sunderland players, management and board. It also specialises in interviews with stars of years gone by and in unearthing stories about the lengths supporters go to in following the lads.

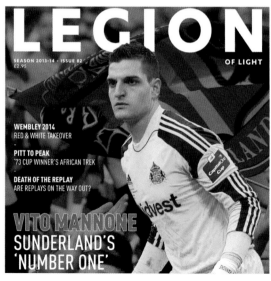

Malone

Leeds reckoned that right back Dick Malone would be the weak link through which they could beat Sunderland in the 1973 FA Cup final. They reckoned wrongly as the man Malone was marking ended up being substituted in those days when only a single sub was allowed.

Malone's direct opponent Eddie Gray was seen as Leeds' match-winner. A brilliant left winger he made a habit of torturing full backs, but Bob Stokoe astutely detailed Bobby Kerr to double up on Gray, and such was the job Malone and Kerr did on their fellow Scot that he was replaced, and with his substitution came admission that Sunderland weren't just outfighting Leeds, they were out-thinking them too.

Dick Malone was a Scotland U23 right back signed from Ayr United in 1970. A tall, gangly player he often looked like he didn't have the ball fully under control but not many could get it off him. The term 'mazy dribble' must have been invented for Malone who the fans christened 'Super Dick' in response to the mag up the road idolised as 'Super Mac'.

Malone made many goals with his forward forays and scored twice himself, one after a 'Malone mazy' and one with a thunderbolt. In seven years at Sunderland, Dick played 282 times before joining Hartlepool and later linking up again with Bob Stokoe and Bobby Kerr at Blackpool. A leading member of the Former Players' Association, Dick also works behind the scenes as a matchday host in the Stadium of Light corporate areas.

Managers

Thomas Watson	3/6/1889 – 17/8/1896	George Hardwick	14/11/1964 – 1/5/1965
Robert Campbell	17/8/1896 – May 1899	Ian McColl	21/5/1965 – 8/2/1968
Alex Mackie	August 1899 to June 1905	Alan Brown	9/2/1968 – 1/11/1972
Fred Dale★	4/11/1904 – 31/1/1905	Billy Elliott^★★	1/11/1972 – 29/11/72
Bob Kyle	August 1905 to 5/5/1928	Bob Stokoe	29/11/1972 – 18/10/1976
Johnny Cochrane	5/5/1928 – 3/3/1939	Ian MacFarlane★★	18/10/1976 – 30/11/1976
George Crow ★★	3/3/1939 – 24/3/1939	Jimmy Adamson	30/11/1976 – 25/10/1978
Bill Murray^	24/3/1939 – 26/6/1957	Dave Merrington★★	25/10/1978 – 11/12/1978
Alan Brown	30/7/1957 – 31/7/1964	Billy Elliott^★★	13/12/1978 – 24/5/1979

Ken Knighton	7/6/1979 – 13/4/1981
Mick Docherty^★★	13/4/1981 – 12/6/1981
Alan Durban	12/6/1981 – 1/3/1984
Pop Robson^★★	1/3/1984 – 5/3/1984
Len Ashurst^	5/3/1984 – 24/5/1985
Lawrie McMenemy	11/7/1985 – 16/4/1987
Bob Stokoe	16/4/1987 - 30/5/1987
Denis Smith	30/5/1987 – 30/12/1991
Malcolm Crosby+	30/12/1991 – 1/2/1993
Terry Butcher^	5/2/1993 – 26/11/1993
Mick Buxton	26/11/1993 - 29/3/1995
Peter Reid++	29/3/1995- 7/10/2002
Howard Wilkinson	10/10/2002 – 10/3/2003
Mick McCarthy	12/3/2003 – 6/3/2006
Kevin Ball^★★	6/3/2006 – 8/5/2006
Kevin Richardson★★	7/7/2006 – 24/7/2006

Niall Quinn^	24/7/2006 – 28/8/2006
Roy Keane	29/9/2006 – 4/12/2008
Ricky Sbragia	4/12/2008 – 24/5/2009
Steve Bruce	3/6/2009 – 30/11/2011
Eric Black	30/11/2011 – 3/12/2011
Martin O'Neill	3/12/2011- 30/3/2013
Paolo Di Canio★★★	31/3/2013 – 22/9/2013
Kevin Ball★★	22/9/2013 – 8/10/2013
Gus Poyet★★★	8/10/2013 to date

★ Caretaker while Alex Mackie suspended.

★★ Caretaker

^ Also played for Sunderland.

+ Caretaker until 29/4/1992, a fortnight before the FA Cup final he'd reached.

++ Caretaker until 22/5/995

★★★ Di Canio and Poyet were appointed as head coach rather than as manager.

For the first three months of the 1964–65 season the team was picked by the directors.

Montgomery

Jimmy Montgomery's total of 627 competitive appearances for Sunderland is 169 more than any other player.

World renowned for his simply brilliant double save from Trevor Cherry and Peter Lorimer in the 1973 FA Cup final, supporters who watched Monty regularly knew that such a save was not particularly unusual for a 'keeper whose ability to make reflex saves was second to none. It was just that this save was on a world stage and in a fantastically important match. While television commentators blathered on thinking Peter Lorimer had scored, before replays proved Monty had kept it out, those in the Sunderland end who hadn't jumped on the bandwagon but had been loyally watching Sunderland week in week out during those dismal early Seventies, simply understood that this was typical Monty.

Born in Sunderland in October 1943, Jim had made his debut a week before his 18th birthday. Capped by England at U23 and youth level it remains a national disgrace that Montgomery never won a full cap. He was around at the same time as the brilliant Gordon Banks but there were plenty of occasions when other 'keepers not as good as Monty got an opportunity. The nearest Monty came was as a reserve in a one sided 5-0 home win over France in 1969.

It was as an unused sub that Jim won

the 'other' major medal of his career. His former Sunderland team mate Brian Clough had taken him to Forest as cover for Peter Shilton and so as a veteran Monty picked up a European Cup winner's medal in 1979 without ever playing a first team game for Forest.

The only player to be a part of both the 1964 promotion team and 1973 cup winning team, Jim's final first team game for Sunderland came at Old Trafford in 1976, 15 years and two days after his debut. It is astonishing to think that despite his massive total Monty's final appearance was three days before his 33rd birthday. Goalkeepers mature with age and although Jim returned in 1980 he never played first team football in his

second spell at Sunderland.

Monty is now the club's official ambassador attending many events at home and abroad. In 2013 the club staged a 'This Is Your Life' evening for Jim who on that evening had the Stadium of Light's largest Conference & Banqueting hall renamed as The Montgomery Suite.

Opposite: *Bob Stokoe with Jimmy Montgomery*

Above: *Monty: This is Your Life*

Most Appearances for Sunderland

Jimmy Montgomery	627		Kevin Ball	375 + 13
Len Ashurst	452 + 6		Johnny Mapson	383
Ted Doig	457		Shaun Elliot	363 + 5
Stan Anderson	447		Martin Harvey	353 + 5
Gary Bennett	434 + 9		Ernie England	352
Bobby Kerr	419 + 14		Cec Irwin	349 + 3
Charlie Buchan	411		Arthur Bridgett	348
Gordon Armstrong	393 + 23		Len Shackleton	348
Michael Gray	383 + 27		Bill Murray	328
Charlie Hurley	400 + 1			
Bobby Gurney	390			

★ Figures include all competitions including minor competitions such as the Anglo-Italian and Anglo-Scottish cups.

Most Goals

Player	Era	League	Cups/Other	Total
Bobby Gurney	1925-1939	205	23	228
Charlie Buchan	1911-1925	209	13	222
Dave Halliday	1911-1925	156	9	165
George Holley	1904-1915	150	9	159
Johnny Campbell	1889-1897	136	18	154
Kevin Phillips	1997-2003	113	17	130
Raich Carter	1930-1939	118	10	128
Jamie Millar	1890-1904	107	19	128
Arthur Bridgett	1903-1912	107	8	115
Patsy Gallacher	1927-1938	100	7	107
Gary Rowell	1976-2004	88	15	103
Len Shackleton	1948-1957	97	3	100

Nine-One

Newcastle United 1-9 Sunderland. Division One. December 5th 1908.

Sunderland's record league victory (11-1 in the FA Cup v Fairfield, Feb 2nd 1895, is the overall record) and still never surpassed as a top flight away win by any club. Sunderland couldn't have picked a better game to go goal crazy could they?

The odd thing is that Newcastle finished as league champions in this season with Sunderland third, but on this particular afternoon the Magpies were well and truly stuffed. The game turned on a controversial decision to give Newcastle a penalty on the stroke of half time. Home debutant Albert Shepherd equalised leaving the visitors somewhat miffed as the whistle went for the break.

It took Sunderland two minutes of the second half to re-take the lead courtesy of Seaham-born George Holley. It was the first of eight goals Sunderland smacked Newcastle with in probably the best half hour in the history of the club. With 13 minutes left Sunderland 'declared' with both Holley and Billy Hogg having hat tricks to their names; Arthur Bridgett with two and another from Jackie Mordue also on the score-sheet.

Sunderland's goals came in the, 8th, 47th, 58th, 62nd, 67th, 69th, 71st, 73rd and 77th minutes.

Nosworthy

'Nugsy' to one and all, owing to his father giving him the nickname as a child because 'he thought my head was shaped like a nugget', Nyron Nosworthy was never far from the top of the popularity charts on Wearside.

Signed on a free transfer from Gillingham following Sunderland's promotion to the top flight in 2005 it was a case of 'Nyron who?' to most supporters. Brought in to provide back up to Stephen Wright, Nosworthy was pitched straight into the action when Wright was injured in the opening game of the season.

Londoner Nosworthy never gave less than 100% and drew comparisons with 1973 FA Cup right back Dick Malone due to his unorthodox style and penchant for occasionally trying the outrageous and getting away with it.

Mid way through Roy Keane's first season in charge Nosworthy was switched to centre back where he made such an impact he was named 'Player of the Year' in a promotion season, his central defensive partner Johnny Evans (on loan from Man Utd) collecting the 'Young Player of the Season' award.

Below: Nyron Nosworthy

Oldest Players

1	Thomas Urwin	39 years 76 days	v Preston N.E.	22 April 1935
2	Bryan `Pop' Robson	38 years 183 days	v Leicester City	12 May 1984
3	Steve Bould	37 years 280 days	v Manchester City	23 August 2000
4	Charlie Parker	37 years 204 days	v Leeds United	13 April 1929
5	Dwight Yorke	37 years 159 days	v Manchester United	11 April 2009

Ord

' Who needs Cantona when we've got Dickie Ord?' as the fans' song used to go. Richard Ord was out of a similar mould to that of Dick Malone and Nyron Nosworthy. A local lad whose debut came in a 7-0 win over Southend in 1987, Ord's best position was at centre back although he could also play in midfield and had lengthy spells at left back.

Only 17 when he broke into the first team, Ord became an England U21 international and amassed 284 appearances in red and white. A fringe player in the 1990 promotion team he was a regular when the equivalent of the Championship was won six years later.

Ord's later years were hampered by

Above: *Dickie Ord*

injury. He missed his own testimonial match and then following a big money move to QPR in 1998 sustained a serious knee injury in his first game and had to retire. In 2012 Dickie released his autobiography written with Andrew Smithson.

Phillips

The only Englishman to have won the European Golden Shoe as the continent's top scorer, Superkev struck 30 Premiership goals in 36 appearances during 1999-2000. With 130 goals Phillips is Sunderland's record post war goal-scorer. Signed as a virtual unknown from Watford, he scored on his debut in the first competitive game at the Stadium of Light. From then on there was no stopping the 'Hitchin Hotshot' who enjoyed a seemingly telepathic understanding with Niall Quinn and superb service from wingers Nicky Summerbee and Allan Johnston.

A goal before he limped off in the Play Off final at Wembley in 1988 made it 35 in his first season, beating Brian Clough's post war seasonal record. Despite missing three months of the next campaign Kevin collected 25 goals in 31 games as a record 105 points were won.

His European golden shoe season made Phillips the first Sunderland player to bag 30 top flight goals since Gurney and Carter both achieved the feat in the 1936 title winning season. Capped eight times by England, the second of his international appearances came at the Stadium of Light in 1999 in a friendly against Belgium.

Phillips' Top Goals

Opposite: *Phillips celbrates a goal*

Kevin Phillips scored 130 goals for Sunderland making him far and away the club's highest post-war scorer. Phillips was the perfect goal-poacher so many of his goals were 'right place – right time' close range finishes which look so simple except for the fact that you have to have the invaluable knack of knowing where the right place at the right time is going to be.

For all the fact that many of Superkev's strikes were simple ones Phillips scored many memorable goals. How's this for a top 10? Which ones would you have that aren't in this list and what would be the order of your top 10?

1) V Newcastle United, August 25th 1999. Sensational derby matchwinner where he chipped the 'keeper in torrential rain.

2) V Chelsea, December 4th 1999, 30 yard screamer, one of a brace in a 4-1 win. The goal made the credits of ITV's highlights programmes the following season.

3) V Charlton Athletic, May 25th 1998. The goal at Wembley in the Play Off final that was Superkev's 35th of the season and broke Brian Clough's post war record of goals in a season.

4) V Bury, April 13th 1998, A curler that was one of four Phillips scored at Gigg Lane on the night promotion was mathematically secured in the record breaking 105 point season.

5) V Barnsley, April 16th 1998, Another trademark curler from the edge of the box before a live TV audience tuning in to see who this brilliant goal-scorer about to be unleashed on the Premiership was.

6) V QPR, January 9th 1999, Comeback volley in front of adoring away support. Kevin had missed almost four months through injury but was back with a bang.

7) V Watford, August 10th 1999, Another from the catalogue of trademark curlers into the top scorner from the edge of the box. This one was combined with a penalty as Phillips scored both goals in Sunderland's first top flight win after promotion.

8) V Aston Villa, October 18th 1999. Clinical header from a Stefan Schwarz cross. Phillips' second of the game in a 2-1 win and a perfect illustration of the fact he could be lethal in the air as well as on the deck despite not being the biggest. Once again timing was the essential skill.

9) V Newcastle Utd. February 5th 2000. The perfect example of Superkev's partnership with Niall Quinn, Phillips latching onto a Quinn flick on to clinically convert. Just for good measure Superkev soon slipped the ball through Magpie 'keeper Steve Harper's legs to pull Sunderland level from 0-2 down, only the final whistle rescuing the visitors who were on the ropes after Phillips brace.

10) V Middlesbrough, February 22nd 2003. A 'Superkev Special' that was the last of Phillips goals for Sunderland.

Pitt

As a 17-year-old in 1969, Ritchie Pitt would mark the biggest names in top flight football and the following morning turn up to be part of the church choir at Ryhope St. Paul's. Replacing Charlie Hurley was indeed a task that may have required help from above.

A schoolboy England international and member of Sunderland's 1969 FA Youth Cup winning team, Pitt had been a regular for two seasons but was out of the side when Bob Stokoe arrived at Sunderland late in 1972. Pitt had lost his place when caretaker manager switched Dave Watson from centre forward to centre half and when Stokoe brought in defender David Young from Newcastle, Pitt's position at the club was in jeopardy especially with Arsenal showing an interest.

Injury to Young let Pitt back in and once in Ritchie didn't look back. Famously he made the first contribution in the cup final, felling England striker Allan Clarke in lumberjack fashion. The message to Leeds was clear: you may be notorious for mixing it but Sunderland aren't here for a day out. The lads meant business. Alongside Dave Watson, Pitt was a tower of strength in the heart of the Sunderland defence.

Cruelly just four games into the following season Pitt was injured, never to play again. Colliding with Luton's John Ryan at the Fulwell End of Roker Park, Ritchie's playing career was over a fortnight before his 22nd birthday. It was his 145th appearance.

Pitt carved out a successful teaching career and became the Chairman of Sunderland's Former Players' Association.

Play Offs

Sunderland don't do play offs, at least not the modern version. The club have been involved in the best known of all play off games, have benefited from perhaps the biggest slice of play off fortune, won perhaps the most important derby ever and yet Sunderland's tale of play offs is essentially one of the deepest misery.

In the nineteenth century, Sunderland participated in what were called Test Matches. These were the Victorian equivalent of play offs, and in 1897 victory over Newton Heath (later to become Manchester United) retained Sunderland's top flight status.

When the play offs reared their head again in the 1980s Sunderland sunk to their lowest ever point – relegation to football's third tier – after somehow being relegated on the away goals rule despite having identical scorelines in both legs of the play off tie with Gillingham. Each side won their home game 3-2 but as Sunderland were at home in the second leg extra time was played on Wearside. Both teams scored once more and Sunderland went down after an aggregate score of 6-6. How was that allowed to happen?

If Sunderland got the rough end of what looks like ill thought out rules in 1987 they certainly saw 'luck' even itself out three years later. After beating Newcastle 2-1 on aggregate at the semi final stage the lads lost 1-0 to Swindon at Wembley. They were

comprehensively outplayed and had it not been for 'keeper Tony Norman having a blinder they'd have been hammered. However when Swindon were found guilty of long rumoured financial irregularities Sunderland found themselves promoted instead.

Eight years later Sunderland were back in the play off final, this time against Charlton. 90 points had not been enough to secure automatic promotion and after a humdinger of a semi with Sheffield United, Peter Reid's team traded eight goals with Charlton before losing 7-6 on penalties when Michael Gray became the first player to fail to score. The game was voted Wembley's greatest but Sunderland had hit the back of the net 10 times and still not won.

Penalties were Sunderland's Achilles heel again in 2004 when a controversial last minute equaliser by Crystal Palace resulted in extra time and penalties which again undid Sunderland's hopes.

Poom

Mart Poom scored as good a headed goal as Charlie Hurley, Dave Watson, Kenwyne Jones or any other Sunderland player has ever done…but 'The Poominator' was playing in goal!

In best 'I'll be back' fashion, Poom was up against his former club Derby, one he'd given great service to. Sunderland had dominated the game only to concede the first goal with just a couple of minutes left. Deep into injury time Sunderland were awarded a corner. As the ball came over the watching 22,535 crowd, each took a double take. There rising to meet the ball, without breaking his stride after running from his own box, was the light blue clad goalkeeper Mart Poom. A split second later Poom's header bulleted into

the net. Normally a goal is greeted with an instant roar but despite Sunderland's usual large travelling support the goal was greeted with stunned silence. It was like the pause that precedes applause at the end of an especially poignant play. Time stood still for a second or two and then the roars came, roars from those that had just seen one of football's great moments.

Ever the ultimate professional the Estonian international was already racing back to his position in goal, refusing to celebrate out of respect for his former club and its fans. The final whistle went immediately however, leaving Poom to take phenomenal applause from both sets of supporters.

Porterfield

Ian Porterfield deserves to be remembered for much more than simply being the goalscorer in the 1973 FA Cup final. A tremendously talented creative midfielder who had the vision to spot a pass and the ability to deliver it, 'Porter' gave excellent service to Sunderland between December 1967 and July 1977, making 268 appearances despite two long spells out of the side, the second after fracturing his skull 18 months after the cup final.

Sunderland legends Charlie Hurley and Len Ashurst both signed him for Reading and Sheffield Wednesday respectively. In due course Ian followed them along the managerial route. Beginning at Rotherham his managerial career included succeeding Alex Ferguson at Aberdeen, becoming the newly formed Premiership's first sacking when relieved of his duties at Chelsea and a globe trotting career that took in Zambia, Saudi Arabia, Oman, Trinidad and Tobago (where he gave Carlos Edwards his international debut), South Korea and finally Armenia whom he led to their greatest ever results beating Poland and holding Portugal during the Euro 08 qualifiers.

On September 11th 2007 Ian lost a hard fought battle with cancer. Tributes paid to him by SAFC, his colleagues from 1973 and the wider football world illustrated just how much impact Porterfield had made with a world famous goal followed by a worldwide contribution to spreading the love of the game.

Poyet

Arriving as head coach at Sunderland in the autumn of 2013 Gus Poyet somehow found a miracle to lift Sunderland from being marooned at the foot of the table to mid-table safety with a game to spare while reaching the final of one cup and quarter final of another along the way. Such a start made Poyet a favourite with the people of Sunderland who warmed to the new style of possession football he brought to the club.

Born in Uruguay in 1967 Poyet moved to Europe as a youngster but failed to find success in France with Grenoble and returned to his homeland to make his name with River Plate in Montevideo (Not the Argentinian club of the same name in Buenos Aires). Returning to Europe with Real Zaragoza he found fame in Spain.

1995 proved to be a high point for Gus who won the European Cup Winners' Cup and the Copa del Rey as well as the Copa America with Uruguay with him being voted the best player in his position in the tournament.

Poyet moved into English football with Chelsea in 1997 becoming a firm favourite and winning the European Cup Winners' Cup again in 1998, scoring in the semi final. Two years later he'd net twice in the semi final of the FA Cup against Newcastle United en route to winning the trophy by defeating Aston Villa in the final.

At the age of 33 Poyet moved across

the capital to Spurs in 2001, playing in the League Cup final a year later alongside Mauricio Taricco who in due course would become his assistant when he became head coach at Brighton and then Sunderland. Poyet's progress to head coach status followed spells at Swindon Town and Leeds United as a coach and a stint as first team coach back at Spurs who he helped guide to the League Cup with a final victory over his former club Chelsea.

A promotion winner in his first year as head coach with Brighton when he was named League One Manager of the Year Gus led The Seagulls to the championship play offs before moving to Sunderland.

Quinn

Charlie Hurley took the award as Sunderland's first Player of the Century but with the club's second century into its middle third it is difficult to think of a likelier candidate to be hailed as the champion of the club's second century than Niall Quinn.

Quinn was Sunderland's record signing when his former Manchester City manager Peter Reid paid £1.3m for him, as Sunderland prepared for their first ever Premiership season in 1996. Quinny promptly scored twice on his full debut as Sunderland registered a first Premiership win, 4-1 away to Forest. Injury quickly curtailed Niall's first season although he came back when nowhere near fit to help earn a point at Newcastle after over six months out.

Scoring the first ever goal and also the first hat trick at the Stadium of Light wrote Niall's name into the record books and once Kevin Phillips arrived to play off him Quinn enjoyed an Indian summer to his career. As well as creating chances galore for Superkev, Niall notched 17 himself in the first season at the Stadium of Light becoming the first Sunderland player to score twice in a game at Wembley. He added a 'third' in that 1998 play off final penalty shoot out but even more importantly is known to have rallied the troops on the way home instilling in them the belief that came through next time round when a record 105 points was achieved.

That season saw Quinn score 21 times to help Sunderland into the Premiership where he proceeded to score in successive St. James' wins as Sunderland regained 'Cock o the North' status. At the apex of that era Niall shared the goals

Above: *Quinn of Sunderland in action during a FA Carling Premier League match*

with Superkev as Chelsea were played off the park, the Black Cats being 4-0 up in 38 minutes with Quinn destroying World Cup winner Desailly who was pleased to be subbed.

Awarded a Benefit Match between Sunderland and the Republic of Ireland just prior to the 2002 World Cup, Niall

played part of the game for each side and donated the £1m raised to hospitals in Sunderland and his native Dublin.

Retiring through injury after Howard Wilkinson's first match as manager, Quinn said thank you to the fans by donating a car to be given away as a prize in the next home match programme. When he returned just under four years later it wasn't a car he was giving supporters but a ride on his 'magic carpet.'

Niall had seen Sunderland sink from the heights of the Reid era to setting an all time low Premiership points tally, clambering back up only to slide straight back down with an even more embarrassing 15 points. He wasn't from

Above: *Niall celebrates*

Sunderland but admitted Sunderland had got under his skin. A man who can charm the birds from the trees, Niall assembled a group of backers called The Drumaville Consortium and bought out long standing chairman Bob Murray.

Reluctantly appointing himself manager until he could get the man he wanted, Niall started his first season in charge attempting to be chairman and manager. Disastrous results didn't daunt him though and together with his backers Quinn pulled off a massive coup in persuading Roy Keane to take up his first managerial post and Quinn's magic carpet ride was cleared for take off.

Niall handed over the chairmanship of the club to Ellis Short on 3rd October 2011 to take over a role as Director of International Development prior to leaving the club on 20th February 2012. The sportsbar at the Stadium of Light is now named Quinn's in Niall's honour and he should never ever have to buy a pint in Sunderland again.

Quotes

Niall Quinn, Former chairman, manager and player.

"I learned my trade at Arsenal, became a footballer at Manchester City, but Sunderland got under my skin, I love Sunderland."

Raich Carter, 1937 FA Cup final captain.

"This was my home town; these were my own folk. I was the local boy who had lead the team to victory and brought home the cup for which they had been waiting for fifty years. What more could any man ask?"

Jimmy Montgomery. SAFC's all time record appearance maker.

"Every time I walk around the place people still want to talk football and that's the beautiful thing."

Kevin Phillips, SAFC's record post war scorer.

"I never knew football fans could be so vocal and fanatical until I came to the North East."

Len Shackleton, 'The Clown Prince of Soccer' who Sunderland signed from Newcastle.

"I'm not biased when it comes to Newcastle. I'm not bothered who beats them"

Ian Porterfield, scorer of the only goal in the 1973 FA Cup final.

"Even as I connected I knew it was a goal. The shot was true and straight as an arrow and our fans penned behind Harvey's goal, must have seen it all the way, they went mad!"

Brian Clough, Former Sunderland player who became a legendary manager.

"I had the quickest 250 league goals

Right: *Raich Carter, immediately behind the Preston keeper, scores Sunderland's second goal in the 1937 FA Cup final*

ever scored, a career record of 251 in 274 matches, eat your heart out Jimmy Greaves, Ian Rush, Gary Lineker, Alan Shearer."

Charlie Buchan, Sunderland's record league goalscorer.

"Well, that 1912 to 1913 season with Sunderland brought me most of my heart's desires. I played in most of the matches and scored 31 league goals. I also collected 11 medals during that wonderful nine months, one of them presented by the Athletic News to the best team of the season."

Trevor Ford, Wales international centre-forward, a record signing when bought in 1950.

"I'm going to introduce you to another Roker Park nickname. It is, in my opinion, more allied to the truth because it is based on the heartbreaks, the frustration and human suffering of a string of players. The tag: 'Centre-forwards' Graveyard'. Since the war more centre-forwards have 'bit the dust' playing for Sunderland than any club I know."

Red & White

Southampton, Sheffield United, Stoke City, Exeter, Lincoln and Cheltenham all sport red and white stripes. Sunderland though have won more than those clubs combined. Sunderland are synonymous with red and white stripes.

Red & White is the name of SAFC's official match programme produced at each home game and always including exclusive columns from the head coach, the boardroom, skipper and players.

Red & White has won many 'Programme of the Year' awards and prides itself on being written by a team of Sunderland experts for supporters who demand in depth insight into the club that they devote so much effort into supporting so passionately.

Roker Park and Sunderland's Previous Grounds

Sunderland's home from 1898 to 1997 situated about a quarter of a mile from where the Stadium of Light stands, Roker Park holds many memories for generations of Sunderland supporters. Many a tear was shed when the place where supporters' dads, granddads and great granddads had supported the Lads was bulldozed.

The record attendance of 75,118 for a 1933 cup tie with Derby is by some 7000 the biggest ever recorded in the north east but it is believed to have been surpassed in 1964 when the gates were pulled down by supporters unable to gain admission for a cup tie with Manchester United.

It was a cup tie against Manchester City in 1973 which was named Roker's greatest game when the ground closed although had enough people who saw it been around to vote perhaps the 5-4 win over Arsenal in 1935, when the two sides were locked at the top of the league, might have edged even this sensational tie.

Liverpool bookended Roker Park, being the first and last visitors, Sunderland winning both games 1-0; Jim Leslie scoring the stadium's first goal and John Mullin the last. More than anything though Roker Park was renowned for its sound: The Roker Roar.

Between their formation in 1879 and the move to Roker Park in 1898 Sunderland played at numerous grounds

all of which are now identified at their sites by the presence of historical blue plaques.

The first ground was at The Blue House Field in Hendon which was used until 1882. While looking for another place to play Sunderland played at a pitch near 'The Cedars' in Sunderland before settling at Groves Field in the Ashbrooke area of Sunderland. Only four games are recorded as being played on this ground used in 1882-83 before Sunderland moved from their starting point on the south side of the river to move northwards never to return.

The first ground north of the river was in Roker but not at Roker Park. A ground at Horatio Street, often known as 'The Dolly Field' was home to the club in 1883-84. In those days a pub called

The Wolseley was used as the changing rooms. You can still have a drink here today as you can at Ashbrooke and indeed there is a pub called The Blue House near the original ground in Hendon.

In 1884 Sunderland moved to Fulwell at Abbs Field. This was the first of the club's grounds to be completely enclosed enabling an entrance charge to be taken.

This was also where Sunderland first began to wear red and white instead of their original blue. The strips though were red and white halves. Stripes wouldn't be worn until following the move to Newcastle Road.

In 1886 Sunderland were on the move again, this time to the Newcastle Road ground which is the nearest to the Stadium of Light of all

On the plaque:

Sunderland Association Football Club

BLUE HOUSE FIELD, HENDON

The first home ground of what is now Sunderland A.F.C. Originally called Sunderland and District Teachers' Association, the Club made their home here from its foundation in 1879 until 1881.

Above: *Blue plaques mark the sites of all of Sunderland's former grounds, including this one at the site of the original ground in Hendon.*

the club's former homes. Newcastle Road became the home of the side that became known as 'The Team of All The Talents'. This team won the league title three times in four seasons at Newcastle Road, which also staged a full England international against Wales in 1891. Twelve years were spent at Newcastle Road before the 99 year stint at Roker Park.

Rowell

Above: Gary Rowell is still an avid fan

One of only three players to top a century of goals for Sunderland since WW2, Seaham-born Gary Rowell was top scorer six times at Sunderland and such a hero that despite the fact that he played his last game for the lads in 1984, the chant of 'We all live in a Gary Rowell world' is still regularly heard.

Scoring a hat trick in a 4-1 win at Newcastle in 1979; when he also made the other goal just for good measure, cemented Gary's legendary status. He completed that hat trick with a penalty. There could be no-one better to take it, Rowell placed 25 of the 26 he took right in the corner of the net, giving 'keepers no chance even if they guessed the side he was putting them.

Still a dedicated Sunderland supporter, in recent years Gary has worked as a radio summariser on Sunderland games as well as penning a must read column in the local newspaper 'The Sunderland Echo.'

Samson

Samson is Sunderland's mascot along with his female counterpart Delilah. The pair of course are black cats in line with Sunderland's nickname. Samson and Delilah entertain young supporters before every match. While most fans just see the feline fans on the pitch in the run up to kick off, Samson and Delilah are busy for an hour and a half before every game helping out in the Family Zone.

Situated in the south-east corner of the Stadium of Light the Family Zone is a very popular area where young fans enjoy a range of interactive pre-match activities to make their day at the match a lot more than the 90 minutes of football.

Samson and Delilah also attend many events run by the Foundation of Light and are always on hand to help the next generation of Sunderland supporters know that they have friendly and welcoming faces at the club they belong to.

Shackleton

Known as 'The Clown Prince of Soccer' Len Shackleton was one of the most talented footballers to have played the game. A star of the 1940s and 50s, 'Shack' was a maverick. He would never toe the line, do the orthodox or even play for the team if it didn't suit him. Stories of disputes between Len and his team mates, especially Trevor Ford, are well known and yet 'Shack' is deeply revered by those old enough to have seen him.

Shackleton could do things with a football that cartoonists would rule out as far fetched. Fond of playing one-twos off the corner flag, another party piece was to appear to pass the ball to an opponent only to have put so much back spin on the ball it would come back to Shack like a well trained dog. From time to time he would sit on the ball to show how much time he had.

Only capped five times, Shack mesmerized world champions West Germany to score against them on his final appearance for England. He was altogether too much for the powers that be at the FA. Leaving a blank page in his autobiography entitled 'The average director's knowledge of football' summed up Shack's lack of respect for authority. The scorer of 100 goals for Sunderland in 348 games, Shack had been bought from Newcastle but was typically candid about his lack of divided loyalties: "I'm not biased when it comes to Newcastle, I'm not bothered who beats them"

Following his playing days Shack became a journalist and behind the scenes a great 'fixer' in recommending people for managerial roles.

Sorensen

This great Dane came into English football with Sunderland in 1998, immediately setting a record 29 clean sheets in a season (plus one from reserve Andy Marriott), but his greatest moments were still to come. Becoming Sunderland's most capped international outside the UK and Republic of Ireland by winning the first 27 of his caps for Denmark while on Wearside, Sorensen was an accomplished goalkeeper who played 197 games for the club.

In November 2001 Sunderland looked to have earned a second successive 2-1 win away to Newcastle only for the home side to be awarded a penalty. Up stepped Tyneside talisman Alan Shearer who claimed so many of his record number of Newcastle goals from the spot. The penalty was well struck but flinging himself low to his left Sorensen saved sensationally, Sunderland went on to win and the image of Shearer left with his head in his hands was indelibly etched into the mind of every Sunderland supporter.

Stadium of Light

The Sunderland Stadium of Light was the biggest football ground built in England in the second half of the twentieth century. Originally it had a capacity of 42,000, since extended to 49,000 and has the potential to be further extended to 55,555 and ultimately to close to 70,000 if required.

Named as the only British ground amongst the top 10 grounds in the world by Total Football magazine shortly after it opened, the stadium has twice been used by England and would be expected to be a key stadium were England to stage a future world cup. Indeed when England bid to host the 2018 FIFA World Cup, the Stadium of Light was the first to be announced as being accepted as a candidate host venue.

Incorrectly believed by some to be named after Benfica's Stadium of Light, the Sunderland Stadium of Light is thus named because of the city of Sunderland's place in the development of light. Joseph Wilson Swan, the inventor of the incandescent light bulb was born near the site of the stadium, Sir Humphrey Davy invented the miners' safety lamp (The Davy Lamp) in the Durham coalfield the site of the Stadium of Light was once part of, and just below the Stadium of Light on the riverside are the remains of lime kilns indicating the limelight Sunderland see themselves as being part of. Benfica's stadium name is simply because the ground is in an area called Luz and in Portuguese Luz means light.

Stadium of
Light Concerts

Right:
*Springsteen at the
Stadium of Light*

2009 Oasis,
       Take That (x two nights)

2010 P!nk

2011 Take That (x four nights)
       Kings of Leon

2012 Bruce Springsteen
       Coldplay
       Red Hot Chili Peppers

2013 Rihanna
       Bon Jovi
       North East Live headlined by
       JLS

2014 One Direction
       North East Live headlined by
       Jessie J

Stokoe

K nown as 'The Messiah' at Sunderland for taking the club back to the promised land of success, Bob Stokoe transformed a team struggling at the foot of the old second division into FA Cup winners in less than six months. Stokoe inherited the nucleus of the team from Alan Brown but he injected it with belief and added some experienced ingredients to get the blend just right.

Once the magic potion had been discovered, miracles started to happen. The best sides in the land weren't just beaten, they were swept aside. This wasn't some second division team packing the defence and looking to score on the break, Sunderland were an attacking team that took on Man City, Arsenal and Leeds (not forgetting Notts County, Reading and Luton) and beat them.

A statue of Bob Stokoe now stands proudly outside the Stadium of Light. As a player he'd been a cup winner with Newcastle, as a manager he'd done the rounds, but his place in history is cast as solidly in Sunderland as his statue.

Stokoe took charge of Sunderland in 206 games, winning 95, drawing 51 and losing 60. As well as winning the FA Cup in 1973, he guided the club to the Second Division (Championship) title in 1976 and in 1987 briefly returned in an attempt to clear up the mess left by Lawrie McMenemy.

Talents

'The Team of All The Talents' were the team of the 1890s. This was the team that first made Sunderland great.

- League Champions in three years out of four
- First team to be champions three times
- Beaten only once at home between September 1890 and August 1897
- 100% home wins record in 1891-92
- First team to score 100 goals in a season – in just 30 games, 1892-93
- Last ever winners of the single tier Football League
- First ever winners of the First Division.

Sunderland were given the name 'The Team of All The Talents' by no less a figure than the Founder and President of the Football League and committee member of Aston Villa,

William McGregor. On April 5th 1890 he saw Sunderland slaughter Villa 7–2 in a friendly and stated: "Sunderland had a talented man in every position." This result combined with a series of others led to Sunderland becoming the first club outside the 12 Founder members to join the two-year-old Football League.

As the decade progressed the great names of 'The Team of All The Talents' included captain Hugh Wilson, 'keeper Ted Doig, Jimmy Millar and Johnny Campbell, whose 154 goals mean he still ranks as the fifth highest goal scorer in the club's history.

Above: *A shot of the team from the 1890's. Note the pitch markings.*

Tueart

Whenever Dennis Tueart got the ball people got excited. Something was always likely to happen once he was in possession. Always keen to take on defenders, Tueart was lighting quick, kept close control, could shoot with either foot and was so elastically athletic and well coordinated he could score goals as spectacular as his scissors kick volley for Sunderland at Oxford in 1973 or his bicycle kick for Manchester City against his home town of Newcastle in the League Cup final of 1976.

Tueart had experienced cup final success three years earlier as part of the Sunderland team who had beaten Leeds to win the FA Cup. Having joined Sunderland in the month England won the World Cup, Tueart came through the ranks at Roker and won the FA Youth Cup in 1969.

His 56 goals for Sunderland included one in the club's first ever major European match where he dribbled from the half way line to score in Budapest against Vasas. Tueart played 214 games for Sunderland and earned his first England call up the day after his 1974 move to Man City, eventually winning six caps. He played in America for the New York Cosmos and played in a second FA Cup final in 1981 having returned to City whom he later served as a director.

When his 1973 team mate Ian

Porterfield passed away in 2007, Dennis spoke with eloquence and compassion at Porterfield's memorial service in Sunderland Minster, illustrating that the bond between that cup winning team was a very special one indeed.

Above: *Dennis Tueart*

Urwin

Thomas Urwin is the oldest player ever to play for Sunderland. He was 39 years and 76 days when he played his 55th and final game at Preston on 22nd April 1935. For many years Bryan 'Pop' Robson was generally accepted as Sunderland's oldest player as a result of appearing at the age of 38 years and 183 days in May 1984 at Leicester.

Urwin was an England international signed from Newcastle as a veteran in 1930. Born in Haswell on 5th February 1896 he began his league career with Middlesbrough and so is one of a small band of players to have played for all of the north east's top three clubs. Having managed over 200 games for both 'Boro and the Mags, Urwin made his Sunderland debut at Leeds, three days after turning 34.

On February 1st 1932 he played in an FA Cup 4th round second replay which Sunderland lost against Stoke at Maine Road, Manchester. It was his last appearance of the season and come the summer the 36-year-old's playing days looked to be at an end. However the vastly experienced player remained on the coaching staff and found himself in the right place at the right time when he was suddenly required almost three years later. Not used at all in the 1932-33 or 1933-34 seasons, the 1934-35 campaign had a mere three games to go when Urwin pulled his boots on for one last time.

Sunderland had two away games on Easter weekend. A 2-2 Easter Saturday draw at Birmingham was followed by a trip to Preston on Easter Monday. Still in with a chance of the title Sunderland had to do without their inside and outside lefts Gallacher and Connor who had picked up injuries at St. Andrews, so Urwin was pressed into action one more time. He helped Sunderland to a point and himself to a place in the record books.

Venison

As Sunderland's skipper in the 1985 League Cup final, Barry Venison became the youngest cup final captain ever seen at Wembley. A first teamer since he was 17, Venison was 20 years and 220 days old when he led Sunderland in the final in the absence of suspended skipper Shaun Elliott.

'Venner' collected a loser's medal as Sunderland lost a poor game with Norwich 1-0. He was to have great success later in his career though, winning the league twice and the FA Cup with Liverpool with whom he also reached another League Cup final. Barry also played for Newcastle, Galatasaray in Turkey, Southampton and twice for England. Following his playing days

the man with a wardrobe full of dodgy jackets became a national TV presenter with ITV Sport.

Watson, Dave

Dave Watson won the Man of the Match award in the 1973 FA Cup final and rightly so. For all Leeds' superstars Sunderland had the best player on show and it was Dave Watson. Uncapped at the time he ended up with 65 England caps to illustrate his pedigree in a career where his CV once completed included spells with Manchester City, Southampton and Werder Bremen in Germany.

Watson was Sunderland's first £100,000 signing when Alan Brown bought him from Rotherham as a centre forward. Dave did well up front and was top scorer with 14 league and cup goals in his first full season. However he had originally been a centre half with his first club Notts County and when Alan Brown was sacked late in 1972 the first thing caretaker boss Billy Elliott did was move him back to his original position.

Watson went from being a decent forward to an exceptional defender. Fantastic in the air, strong in the challenge, comfortable on the ball and a good reader of the game, Watson was a class act, a fact he proved in the cup final and for many years to come.

Above: Dave Watson

Watson, Willie

Willie Watson was so good he played for England. So what you might think, lots of players do that. The thing is Willie played for England at both football and cricket! Only 12 people have ever done that with only one of them (Arthur Milton of Arsenal & Gloucestershire) doing so since Watson's feat. Moreover Watson was arguably the most successful of the 'double internationals.'

Watson's international football career commenced when he was part of an England team who thrashed Northern Ireland 9 (nine) – 2 in 1949. A year later he won the third of his four full football caps in an international at Roker Park where Wales (including Willie's Sunderland teammate Trevor Ford) were beaten 4-2.

At cricket Willie played in 23 Test Matches achieving two centuries and three half centuries from his 37 innings, averaging 25.85 from his 879 runs. In First Class cricket overall Willie scored over 25,000 runs with a highest score of 257 and an average of 39.86. He notched 55 centuries and 132 half centuries, holding 295 catches for good measure.

As a footballer the opening 11 games of Watson's career were with Huddersfield where his father had been part of the Huddersfield team who under Herbert Chapman became the first ever club to win the league title three years running. Willie's brother Albert was also

a sportsman, playing for Huddersfield and Oldham, who he captained.

Much of Willie's career was lost to World War Two. His handful of games for Huddersfield came before the war. It was April 1946 when he joined Sunderland for who he played 223 games, mainly as a top class wing half,

scoring 17 goals before becoming player/manager of Halifax Town in 1954.

His native Yorkshire, and then Leicestershire, were Willie's cricketing counties prior to his emigration to South Africa in 1968. Willie Watson, who ran sports shops in Sunderland, died in 2004.

Wickham

When Sunderland produced their 'Greatest Escape' in 2014, evading the clutches of relegation from a seemingly impossible position of being seven points adrift with six tough fixtures to go, it proved to be Connor Wickham who was the main miracle worker.

A fortnight past his 21st birthday Wickham announced his arrival on the big stage with two well taken goals to earn a shock point away to champions elect Manchester City. Three days later he scored the opening goal as Jose Mourinho's 78 match unbeaten home Barclays Premier League record as Chelsea manager was brought to an untimely and unlikely end by bottom of the table Sunderland. Wickham followed that up with two well-taken headers and the winning of a penalty as Cardiff were thrashed. Those five goals in three games helped earn Connor the Barclays Premier League Player of the Month award for April, an accolade he celebrated by turning provider in setting up the winner for Seb Larsson away to Manchester United as Sunderland's meteoric rise continued.

Wickham has long been a player seen as having a bright future. Just 11 days after his 16th birthday he became the youngest player in Ipswich Town's history and while at Portman Road won awards as Football League and Championship Player of the Month, Football League Young Player of the Year and Championship Apprentice

of the Year.

Having scored the winner in the final of the 2008 Victory Shield for England U16s against Scotland, Wickham went further a year later when being named 'Golden Player' at the European U17 championships. In that tournament he scored the winner in the final against Spain after netting both goals to defeat France at the semi final stage. Subsequently he has gone on to play at U19 and U21 level and with a father hailing from Northern Ireland remains eligible for an Irish cap until such time as England cap him at full competitive level.

A big bustling centre forward with pace and the ability to finish, Wickham was seen as an expensive buy when Steve Bruce brought him to the Stadium of Light in the summer of 2011 but after a lengthy wait for a dividend Wickham duly delivered when Sunderland needed a Harry Houdini to escape from the difficulties they found themselves encountering in the spring of 2014.

Women

Right: *SAFC Ladies in action*

Since September 2013 Sunderland Ladies FC have been officially part of Sunderland AFC. Newly accepted into the Women's Super League they played their first WSL game on April 17th 2014 winning a second division match 4-2 away to Durham at New Ferens Park, Abbey Joice claiming Sunderland's inaugural goal.

Sunderland Ladies history stretches back to 1989 and a five a side team called the Kestrels. The club gradually grew and from 2000 enjoyed strong connections with SAFC.

Their success in recent years has been superb. Third in the Women's Premier League Northern Division in 2007-08 they won promotion the following year in a season that also saw them reach the final of the FA Women's Cup, going down by the odd goal in three to Arsenal at Derby County's Pride Park.

From 2011 to 2013 a hat trick of FA Women's National Premier titles was achieved, the FA Women's League Cup also being added to the trophy cabinet in 2012.

World Cup

Sunderland staged a World Cup quarter final and three group games when England staged the World Cup in 1966. The USSR defeated Hungary 2-1 in the quarter final at Roker Park where they had already beaten Italy and Chile, Italy having beaten Chile in Roker's opener.

Soviet 'keeper Lev Yashin, Magyar's maestro Ferenc Bene and Azzuri ace Sandro Mazzola were amongst those starring at Sunderland.

Four decades on the Stadium of Light was earmarked as a probable semi final stadium had England won the right to stage the 2006 tournament. Sunderland was also earmarked as a candidate host city had England won the right to stage the FIFA World Cup in 2018. When the World Cup next comes to English shores perhaps Wearside will again have a role to play.

Sunderland's first connection with the World Cup was Willie Watson's involvement in 1950 when England participated for the first time. Watson wasn't called upon however and so Billy Bingham became the first Sunderland player to actually play in the finals. Bingham represented Northern Ireland in 1958 and managed his country in the 1982 finals. In 2002 the USA's Claudio Reyna was named in FIFA's team of the tournament while on Sunderland's books.

XIs

JIMMY MONTGOMERY
- Record appearance maker
- 1973 FA Cup hero

WARNEY CRESSWELL
- England international
- 1920s stalwart
- 'The Prince of full backs'

CHARLIE HURLEY
- SAFC Player of the Century
- Republic of Ireland international
- Club's most capped player

DAVE WATSON
- 1973 Cup final man of the match
- Club's most capped England appearance maker

LEN ASHURST
- SAFC record outfield appearance maker
- Tough tackler
- 'Lennie the Lion'
- Also managed club

BILLY BINGHAM
- Northern Ireland international
- Star of the 50s

RAICH CARTER
- One of England's greatest players
- Captained 36 champs & 37 cup winners

LEN SHACKLETON
- 'Clown Prince of Soccer'

- England international

JIMMY CONNOR
- Scottish international
- Crowd favourite in 1930s

DAVE HALLIDAY
- Most goals in a season (43)

- More goals in his poorest season than anyone else has scored in their best

BOBBY GURNEY
- Record club scorer (228)
- 31 goals in 36 title win, 1st goal in '37 final

Young

Substitute in the 1973 FA Cup final, David Young wasn't called upon at Wembley but played his part in the cup run playing in the fourth round and fourth round replay with Reading.

Signed from Newcastle along with Ron Guthrie in January '73, Young was a left sided defender who debuted in a 4-0 win over Brighton, the biggest win of the season. Having impressed in his first few games on Wearside, Young was unlucky to lose his place through injury and with his replacement, Ritchie Pitt, looking solid in the heart of the defence alongside Dave Watson, Young found himself twelfth man beneath the twin towers.

Injury ended Pitt's career early the

following season in which Young had a couple of spells in the team but moved on to Charlton in the summer of '74 having played 40 times for Sunderland.

Youngest Players

1	Derek Forster	15 years 185 days	v Leicester City	22 August 1964
2	Jimmy Hamilton	16 years 103 days	v Preston N.E.	25 September 1971
3	Cec Irwin	16 years 166 days	v Ipswich Town	20 September 1958
4	Rob Hindmarch	16 years 262 days	v Orient	14 January 1978
5	Dominic Sharkey	16 years 341 days	v Scunthorpe Utd	9 April 1960

Z Cars

Z Cars was a hugely popular police based TV series of the 60s and 70s. Like 'Dr. Who' of similar vintage part of its appeal was due to its catchy theme tune. The tune which came from the traditional folk song, 'Johnny Todd', became the music Sunderland ran out to in the 1960s and it still accompanied the team's entrance during the 1973 cup winning run. Used by Everton as well, the Toffees still run out to it.

On the occasion of the tribute to the cup final goal scorer, Ian Porterfield, following his death in September 2007, the rest of the 1973 team requested that Sunderland's Stadium of Light entrance music

(Prokofiev's 'Dance of the Knights' from Romeo & Juliet followed by U2s 'Elevation') was replaced by 'Z Cars' for the day.

The sound of Z Cars heralding the arrival of the Lads was lost on younger generations but to those who were there when Stokoe's Stars brought about the biggest dose of cup fever Sunderland - and probably anywhere else – has ever seen, Z Cars was undeniably the theme tune.

The pictures in this book were provided courtesy of the following:

GETTY IMAGES
101 Bayham Street, London NW1 0AG

WIKICOMMONS
commons.wikimedia.org

Design and artwork by Scott Giarnese

Published by G2 Entertainment Limited

Publishers Jules Gammond and Edward Adams

Written by Rob Mason